Ethics at Work

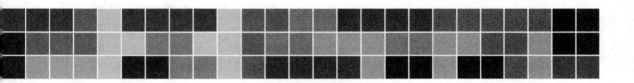

ROBERT W. HUNT

with

MATTHEW B. HUNT

BARBARA G. COX

NETEFFECT SERIES

PEARSON

Prentice
Hall

Upper Saddle River, New Jersey

Library of Congress Cataloging-in-Publication Data

Hunt, Robert.
  Ethics at work / Robert W. Hunt, Matthew B. Hunt,
Barbara G. Cox.
    p. cm. – (NetEffect series)
  Includes index.
  ISBN 0-13-045031-6
  1. Business ethics.   I. Hunt, Matthew B. II. Cox, Barbara G.
III. Title. IV. Series.
  HF5387.H862 2005
  174–dc22

2004002638

> *For
> Nancy Hunt—
> the best person
> I have ever known*

Editor-in-Chief: Stephen Helba
Director of Production and Manufacturing: Bruce Johnson
Executive Editor: Elizabeth Sugg
Editorial Assistant: Cyrenne Bolt de Freitas
Marketing Manager: Leigh Ann Sims
Managing Editor—Production: Mary Carnis
Manufacturing Buyer: Ilene Sanford
Production Liaison: Denise Brown
Full-Service Production: Gay Pauley/Holcomb Hathaway
Composition: Carlisle Communications, Ltd.
Design Director: Cheryl Asherman
Senior Design Coordinator/ Cover Design: Christopher Weigand
Director, Image Resource Center: Melinda Reo
Manager, Rights and Permissions: Zina Arabia
Interior Image Specialist: Beth Brenzel
Cover Image Specialist: Karen Sanatar
Image Permission Coordinator: Charles Morris
Cover Printer: Phoenix Color
Printer/Binder: RR Donnelley & Sons

Pearson Prentice Hall™ is a trademark of Pearson Education, Inc.
Pearson® is a registered trademark of Pearson plc
Prentice Hall® is a registered trademark of Pearson Education, Inc.

Pearson Education Ltd.
Pearson Education Singapore Pte. Ltd.
Pearson Education Canada, Ltd.
Pearson Education—Japan

Pearson Education Australia Pty. Limited
Pearson Education North Asia Ltd.
Pearson Educación de Mexico, S. A. de C.V.
Pearson Education Malaysia Pte. Ltd.

10 9 8 7 6 5 4
ISBN 0-13-045031-6

Contents

8 Corporate Character and the Role of Leadership   85

Preface

Tell a friend or neighbor that you are working on a book about ethics in business, and the response—unless they think you're a scoundrel—is liable to be something like, "It's about time someone did," or "Goodness knows, it's needed." Tell a person who is in the business of teaching business ethics, and the response is more likely to be, "Why add another one to the field?"

There are many excellent books on the topic of ethics in business. Some of those books are written by professionals (i.e., professors of ethics or business) for professionals. Some are written by professionals for laypeople. Some are written by laypeople for fellow laypeople. And some books are written for students in courses on business ethics.

Ethics at Work is written for readers who are, or may expect to be, in the business world. It presumes that the readers will not have previously taken an ethics course. In that sense, it is *introductory.* This book aims to provide the reader with material (ideas, manners of reasoning, ways of looking at things—"tools," if you will) that will assist him or her in making ethical decisions, and becoming a better person.

Not that this book will make good guys out of bad guys. No ethics book can do that on its own. Golf lessons for someone who doesn't care about playing golf won't accomplish much either. But, if the reader comes to this book with the willingness to improve his or her ability to live and act ethically in an often complex and challenging work environment, then this book should help—it is meant to help—in achieving that goal.

Given the target audience of this book, certain choices were made regarding its style and format.

■ Every attempt was made to present the material in a reader-friendly manner. I have tried to meet the readers where they are—at least where I think they are—rather than to ask, or require, them to enter into a special field of study with its own distinctive setting, structure, and terminology.

■ This book is purposely short on names, dates, labels, and -isms. The reader will encounter some classical ethical viewpoints, to be sure, but the aim here is not to teach the *history* of ethics. Personally, I believe that names, dates, and labels will likely distract from the issues at hand, but reasonable people may disagree about that.

■ *Ethics at Work* begins by considering a number of theoretical and meta-ethical issues (though it certainly doesn't say it that way), and then moves on both to normative ethics and to a version of virtue ethics. A companion work, the *Participant's Guide*, consists of scenarios and exercises that give readers the opportunity to put some of these concepts to work. It is not necessary, however, to use the two texts together. *Ethics at Work* itself contains both pre- and post-chapter questions that are meant to engage the reader with respect to the concepts that have been introduced.

■ The book is full of questions. They occur at the beginning and end of each chapter. Moreover, under the rubric "Think About It," they appear throughout the chapters as well. The intent of the chapter "Warm-up" and "Think About It" questions is both to stimulate and to guide thinking. They are questions about the subject matter at hand, but not "about" it in the sense of being test questions to determine whether or not the reader has mastered the material.

The "Wrap-up" questions at the end of each chapter do have correct or "best" answers, based on the content of the chapter. While they could be used as tests, their primary purpose is to help summarize key concepts within the chapters.

A brief word is in order regarding the cartoons in this book. While there has been an attempt to locate them in chapters to which they might have a particular relevance, no one should push this idea too far. The cartoons do not necessarily support or reflect on a specific point of view under discussion. Please, don't ask what they mean or why they are there—just enjoy them. They are for fun. The topic of ethics is serious business, but reading, studying, or talking about it need not be grim.

Ethics at Work is based on the idea that business ethics involves applying general ethical principles to the particular and often complex situations that arise in business. This is a widely, but not universally, held view. There are those who would maintain that business ethics is, in some manner or other, sui generis—that it is not just (*just!*) the application of general ethical principles to business situations. Certainly, an interesting debate can be carried on regarding this matter, but an introductory level book is not the proper venue for that debate. Nor is its preface.

Ethics at Work avoids a particular ethical point of view. Yet one could always argue that the text *does* adopt a position—the position Richard De George has called *moral pluralism*.*

The text presents many points of view through a summary of the analysis it does provide.

> The ethical approaches reviewed here all have strengths and weaknesses. None is perfect. So when you have a tough decision to make, you should look at it from a variety of perspectives (some of which you might not have considered before reading this book), and then *you* have to decide what is going to guide you in that situation. There's no guarantee that you will wind up doing the right thing. But it's more likely that you will, and you will certainly turn out to be a better person—*because you tried to be*—than if you had simply acted without reflection.

If readers come away with a larger and better set of tools for making ethical decisions than they had before, and an increased willingness to use them, then this book will have succeeded.

---

*See *Business Ethics*, 5th ed. (Upper Saddle River, N.J.: Prentice Hall, 1999), 53.

Acknowledgments

Don Messick, Jim Slevcove, and Mike Molus are entrepreneurs and proficient businessmen. They have provided clear examples of the fact that successful businesses can be conducted with integrity, care, and a respect for persons. They have taught me far more, I am sure, than they ever knew they were teaching me.

The contribution of the expert review team needs also to be noted. Many thanks to Professor Michael Moch at Michigan State University and Professor William Tita at Northeastern University.

It has been a privilege and a delight to work on this project with Barbara Cox, Ph.D., and my son, Matt Hunt, Ph.D. Not only colleagues, they are also friends. Both are true educators, and by virtue of their contributions a manuscript has been transformed into a tool for learning. Students and instructors who use this book will owe them much.

Luke Artzer is a good person who could—and should—write the book on sales. He, too, may not have realized how much he was teaching me.

Multiple generations of my family have provided encouragement and exercised patience. For all of that, I am grateful.

Robert W. Hunt
San Clemente, California

Theory and Practice

PERFORMANCE GOALS

After completing this chapter, learners will be able to:

- understand that exercising ethics is a skill that they can improve.
- identify different criteria that might be applied in making an ethical judgment.
- discuss why common understandings of terminology are usually sufficient in the study of ethics.
- indicate why analysis and debate about ethical matters are not different in kind from those about business matters.
- discuss why business ethics is not a unique kind of ethics.

Dilbert reprinted by permission of United Feature Syndicate, Inc.

Warm-Up Questions

Note: These warm-up questions are not "tests" for which there are right and wrong answers. The questions are meant to engage your thoughts about the chapter material and to elicit your *opinions.*

1. "Some people are better at ethics than others."

        Agree   Disagree

2. It has been discovered that a product has a defect that can cause injury. Recalling the product immediately would be the right thing to do

  A. if it would have good PR value.

  B. if it would minimize company liability.

  C. because it would prevent harm.

  D. if the intent of the recall is to protect people from harm.

  E. because the law would require it sooner or later anyway.

  F. All of the above.

  G. None of the above.

3. Categorize each term as one of the following:

  A. term whose meaning is generally agreed upon;

  B. terms that are very likely to have different meanings to different people; or

  C. term that only experts use and understand.

____ hedge fund	____ fair profit	____ fine-tuned
____ satisfactory	____ vertical integration	____ moral duty
____ leveraged buyout	____ mass media	____ tax deductible
____ book value	____ efficient	____ zero sum game
____ marketable	____ integrity	____ depreciable
____ selfish action	____ profit margin	____ good taste

4. In each set of parentheses, circle the word that you think is appropriate to make the sentence true and complete.

"Ethical decisions are (like/unlike) business decisions, because they usually (do/don't) require an analysis of facts. Though sometimes neither of them may be certain, ethical decisions (like/unlike) business decisions (are/are not) almost always subjective or arbitrary."

5. "Companies within industry A typically seek to achieve a 1 percent profit on total dollar sales volume, whereas companies within industry B typically seek to make 2 percent."

Based on this information, for each of the following indicate whether you agree or disagree.

A. Companies within industry B are typically less ethical than companies within industry A.

    Agree   Disagree

B. Companies in both A and B are equally unethical, because you can't try to make a profit and be ethical at the same time.

    Agree   Disagree

C. The amount of profit a company makes has nothing to do with whether or not the company is ethical.

    Agree   Disagree

D. The amount of profit made is one, but only one, factor in determining whether or not a given company is ethical.

    Agree   Disagree

NATURALS

Sometimes people can perform well at one activity or another without even thinking about it. We often call them *naturals*. Some can drive a golf ball, others can draw a picture, and still others can prepare a succulent dish, all, as it were, *effortlessly*. Such people drive the rest of us crazy when we struggle to perform the same tasks at the same level.

At the other end of the spectrum are the poor souls who study, take lessons, analyze, and theorize yet still can't perform very well. (Any golfers out there?) All the lessons and all the study in the world just don't seem to help. They may know everything about the activity in question, but they can't do it. For these people, learning is all in the head; it doesn't improve performance.

Those are the extremes. Most of us fall somewhere in between with regard to the various activities we pursue. We have some natural abilities that afford us a modicum of success, but we also benefit from study and analysis. Learning enhances our performance.

Probably most of us have known someone who was a natural at business: the kind of person who seems to know intuitively how a market will react, the salesman who can sell ice in Antarctica, the negotiator who just *knows* what his counterpart will accept. And we've encountered the other type, too: the MBA who wouldn't recognize a deal if it were staring him in the face, the HR expert who knows nothing about people, etc.

When it comes to business—whatever our business activity may be— most of us probably fall somewhere in the middle. We have some natural talents and inclinations, and we can also benefit from theory and instruction.

Inasmuch as the practice of ethical behavior is a human activity, it should be no surprise that the same kind of spectrum exists. Many of us have been privileged to know people who were naturals at ethics. They just seem to have an intuitive sense of what is good and right. Without benefit of formal analysis and structured training, they can ferret out the morally right course of action in a complex and conflicting situation with the same quick ease that a talented quarterback can step up to the line of scrimmage, read a defense, and pick out the right play to call.

Conversely, most of us have known those at the other end of the spectrum—people who could talk the talk, but did not walk the walk. Too often, we have known such people because they were public figures. They rose to public esteem sometimes precisely because of their moral fluency and their ability to articulate a vision of personal and societal goodness; yet they themselves could not or would not practice what they preached. Their knowledge of morality far outran their ability to practice it.

> *. . . in the activity of ethics most of us probably fall somewhere in between the extremes.*

As with so many things, in the activity of ethics most of us probably fall somewhere in between the extremes. Neither sinners nor saints, we confront our daily situations equipped with a moderate skill set that includes both instincts about and knowledge of what is right and good. We are not utter novices at acting ethically, nor are we unable to do so by virtue of our jobs or our ambitions.

Moreover, as with other activities, most of us can probably benefit—i.e., improve our ethical performance—by the study of ethics and by exposure to considerations and points of view that might not previously have occurred to us.

> *. . . in studying ethics we are likely to find that there is actually more agreement than disagreement . . .*

In this course we may encounter perspectives with which we disagree; but that, of course, can be beneficial. For in articulating our disagreements, we are likely to hone and amplify our own orientation. Of even greater interest, though, is that in studying ethics we are likely to find that there is actually more agreement than disagreement among the various approaches that may be taken. We can learn from this, and we can also be encouraged by it; for we see that the desire to discern and to do what is right is not a solitary venture. It is an activity that occurs within a community, and we may draw on the resources and support of our various communities as we engage in this distinctly human activity.

THINK ABOUT IT . . .

Among people you know personally, who do you think is the most ethical? Do you think ethical behavior is *natural* to them, or was it *learned?* Or both? Do you know anyone who seems to *know* a lot about ethics and being ethical, but who isn't?

EVALUATIONS, JUDGMENTS, AND CRITERIA

The study of ethics involves, among other things, the study of right and wrong, good and bad. Such a study involves a consideration of ethical judgments and codes of behavior, but the intent is not simply to catalog what has been judged as right and what has been judged as wrong. Rather, we seek to know *why* certain things have been judged as ethically right, while others have been judged as wrong. We want to know the criteria by which such judgments are made. We want to know what tests or rules are applied in order to determine whether an action is judged as right or wrong. For when we know *that*, then we will be in a position to evaluate new situations and, by applying the appropriate criteria, to discern what will constitute right action in those situations.

> . . . we seek to know why certain things have been judged as ethically right, while others have been judged as wrong. We want to know the criteria by which such judgments are made.

Sometimes the same evaluation may be supported by quite different criteria: Suppose the Tyke Toy Company immediately and voluntarily issues a product recall of a children's toy, the Beta Ray Blaster, upon discovering that the Beta Ray Blaster could break in a way that is liable to injure the child using it. We might all agree that the recall was the right thing to do, but we might differ considerably as to what made it right.

Some might say it was the right thing to do because the company's quick consumer-oriented response would generate goodwill and customer loyalty that will likely far outweigh the negative consequences of the recall costs. Yet others might argue that this sense of "the right thing" has nothing to do with ethics; it is right only in the sense of a pure business judgment.

Someone else might argue that, regardless of the business perspective, the product recall should be judged as right because, for ethical judgment, the relevant question is whether the action will maximize good consequences and minimize negative ones. Inasmuch as that can be said of this action, it was, ethically, the right thing to do. That it was also a good business decision is just "frosting on the cake" and shows that ethics and good business don't necessarily conflict.

Yet another party might argue that the relevant ethical consideration has to do with the *intentions* of those who made the decision. Sure, it's nice that the action has good results for those potentially affected, but why did the company decide to do what it did? If the intention was merely to advance the company's interest on the basis of a dollars-and-cents cost–benefit analysis, then no positive ethical value attaches to the action at all. However, if the intent behind the Tyke decision was to protect the public, then the ac-

THINK ABOUT IT . . .

Two people each have an opportunity to misappropriate company equipment for their own use. One doesn't do it because the equipment doesn't belong to him. The other doesn't do it because she's afraid she would be caught. Did they both do the right thing?

tion was an ethically correct one. Moreover, says the person who focuses on intent, this would be true regardless of what consequences were produced.

We can see, then, that investigating the criteria by which ethical judgments are made goes to the very heart of ethical studies. If we understand the different considerations that come into play when people make ethical judgments, we are better able both to understand the source of our differences—when there are differences—and also to see how different approaches may be suited for different situations.

TERMINOLOGY

Like a study of any subject, the study of ethics involves terminology, and it is worthwhile to make a few observations about the vocabulary of ethics at the outset.

The good news is that, in large part, we are all already familiar with the terms used in ethical discussion. Ethical judgments, characterizations, and assessments are a common, if not everyday, part of human experience. The language of ethics is not a jargon spoken only by experts. We do not need to learn it as we would the terminology used in some esoteric academic field.

> *The language of ethics is not a jargon spoken only by experts.*

The bad news, however, is a result of the good news. Precisely because the language of ethics is one of common human experience, it is full of terms that are seldom precise, that sometimes overlap, and that often appear to be inter-changeable. We are all familiar with terms like *ethics, morals, good, bad, right, wrong, duty, justice,* etc. We can use them in conversation and apply them as the situation warrants. Yet each of us would quite likely define each word differently; some might despair of defining most of them at all; and all of us probably use them inconsistently from time to time.

This can have an unsettling effect on someone who wishes to embark on a study of ethics. If the terminology is not clear-cut and precise, how can we expect to resolve anything? Won't we always, or at least too often, be at cross-purposes in our attempts to learn and better understand?

Not to worry. We don't have to agree first on the meaning of *is* in order to have a conversation. If we had to agree on precise definitions before engaging in dis-cussion, nothing would ever get said. But that does not imply that we don't really understand each other. Our understanding is generally just fine for the situation at hand; and if we need to clarify or, for the purposes of a particular conversation, define certain terms, we can do that.

> *If we had to agree on precise definitions before engaging in discussion, nothing would ever get said.*

One example: The terms *ethics* and *morals* are often used interchange-ably. Sometimes they are not. On occasion people will try to distinguish them by suggesting that *ethics* have to do with public or professional be-havior, whereas one's *morals* refer to private conduct. At other times prac-tically the opposite is espoused. Some observers use *ethics* to denote private or individual codes of conduct, whereas *morals* (and *morality*) are said to be a matter of cultural or societal norms.

There is no cause for intellectual anxiety over this. If, for the purposes of a particular point or discussion, we need to make a distinction by defin-ing a term in a certain way—perhaps making a word's meaning more pre-cise than it really is—then we can do so, without claiming to legislate a definition for language as a whole. But if the discussion at hand doesn't call for such refinement, we should be perfectly comfortable using some of these vague and occasionally ambiguous terms just as they stand.

The point, after all—and we do well to keep this in mind—is *doing* the right thing, not *saying* the right thing.

THINK ABOUT IT . . .

Most of us at one time or another have engaged in a discussion as to whether or not a particular company policy was fair. Try to recall such a discussion. Do you think the participants meant the same thing by *fair*? Was it necessary to agree on a definition?

REASON AND ARGUMENT IN ETHICS

Some people remain skeptical about the study of ethics because, they say, ethics is not a science, it is not based on fact. Well, yes, we acknowledge that ethics is not rocket science—ethics may be no kind of science at all. But one should not therefore infer that ethics is an intellectual free-for-all, where anything goes and every opinion is as good as any other.

Without engaging in a lot of philosophical mumbo jumbo about what is a fact, we can agree that, in a certain sense, ethical judgments—assertions about what is right, good, just, and dutiful—may not be assertions of fact.

> *You can't verify an ethical judgment the same way you can confirm a statement about the weather.*

You can't verify an ethical judgment the same way you can confirm a statement about the weather. Nonetheless, a serious study of ethics should disabuse students of the notion that ethics is somehow arbitrary, that one ethical opinion is just as good as another.

Certainly we can note without much trouble at all that questions of fact may play an important role in the formation of ethical judgments. Whether or not a given course of action will harm people is a question of fact; and whether a particular benefit will outweigh a known harm is also a question of fact. Such factual questions may not determine our ethical assessments, but they frequently, if not always, play a substantive role in the formation of our ethical conclusions.

In short, you can't be serious about ethics and ignore the realities of the world. Ethical decision making requires a serious investigation of facts and potential consequences as much as an understanding of ethical principles.

> *In short, you can't be serious about ethics and ignore the realities of the world.*

"But how can it be," an earnest critic might ask, "that two different people might both have a Ph.D. in ethics yet still disagree strongly about what is or is not the right thing to do in a given situation? Doesn't this show that there is an arbitrariness to ethics, that it is not like physics or chemistry or—let me say it—rocket science?"

First, the observation is true, but the conclusion is unwarranted. Yes, different people well schooled in ethics may disagree about particular cases. Ethics is not like the settled sciences (acknowledging that there is often much disagreement at the frontiers of *all* the sciences); but that is not to say that it is therefore somehow arbitrary or subjective.

Consider how a well-run corporation might set out to make an important *business* decision. Consult experts, gather facts, sketch scenarios, and apply principles. But, as we know, experts frequently disagree, there are never enough facts, scenarios aren't guaranteed, and principles have been known to conflict. Does this mean that business decisions, then, are necessarily arbitrary and not the products of reason? Not at all. It simply shows that business decisions, *like ethical decisions*, are made in the muck and the mire of the real world and everyday experience. They aren't pristine controlled experiments conducted in the luxury of a laboratory setting. Business decisions may not be based on "science," but they aren't shot from the hip either. It's the same ethics.

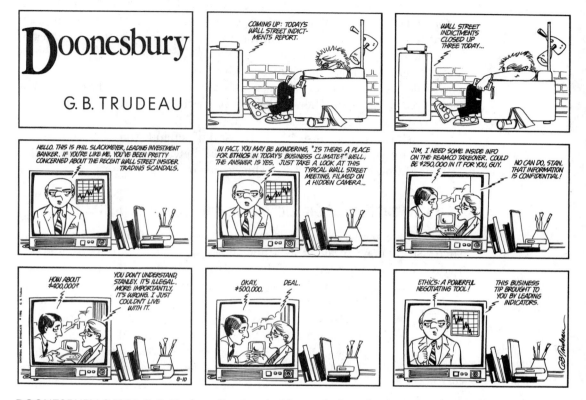

BUSINESS ETHICS

We come now to the topic of business ethics. Does this have to do with some special brand of ethics that is or should be practiced by people who are in business? Are there special ethical rules for the businessperson, companies, and corporations? In general the answer to such questions is "no," although there is a case that calls for an affirmative response.

Not a special kind of ethics, business ethics is simply the application of general ethical approaches and principles within the context of particular business concerns and situations. The study of business ethics is a study of how the norms, rules, and guidelines that may be familiar to us in our personal or nonbusiness activities also apply to our professional and corporate conduct.

> *The study of business ethics is a study of how the norms, rules, and guidelines that may be familiar to us in our personal or nonbusiness activities also apply to our professional and corporate conduct.*

The only sense in which business ethics might be said to be a special kind of ethics, or to involve special kinds of ethical rules, is when an ethical inquiry into particular business contexts leads to the generation of special codes or guidelines for activities within those contexts. Many organizations—both commercial and otherwise—draw up their own set of ethical guidelines for members and employees. It is common, for example, for corporations and government agencies to have ethics rules that prohibit receiving gifts, or gifts above a certain value, from entities with whom they interact professionally. Such rules do not conflict with general ethical principles; indeed, they may be derived from them. They are special or specialized in the sense that they apply only to persons in those positions.

If business ethics is just the application of general ethical principles and considerations, why, it might be asked, is there a need for studies called "business ethics" at all? We'll consider three responses.

1. To Reveal Ethical Dimensions Previously Unrecognized

One often-expressed reason for studying ethics as applied to business is that such a study may reveal ethical dimensions to situations and behaviors that had previously not been recognized. In the heat of a competitive business or professional environment, it is very easy to lose sight of—or never see at all—the fact that one's actions and decisions may have ethical implications, implications that one would not knowingly have ignored. "I never thought of it that way" is a common response when it is pointed out that a particular business decision may, from an ethical point of view, be unacceptable. (Of course, "I don't care" might be another frequently given response to such an observation; but that speaks to other issues.)

> *In the heat of a competitive business or professional environment, it is very easy simply to lose sight of—or never see at all—the fact that one's actions and decisions may have ethical implications . . .*

In recent decades more than one international company has been brought up short by stockholders and customers alike who objected to these organizations outsourcing tasks to people who thought nothing of exploiting underage workers and others. No one *intended* that this would be the case. For the most part, these issues weren't even factored into the decision-making process.

To note this, though, is in no way to single out business as a particularly ethically insensitive field. The same could be said of a variety of other pursuits. Indeed, one of the phenomena that gave rise to the now fully developed field of medical ethics was the growing awareness that medical decisions—many of which were only recently made possible by new technology (think of life-prolonging support systems, egg transplantation, in vitro fertilization, genetic therapy, etc.)—were being made with little or no consideration of the complex ethical issues they involved. This happened not because bad people were making the decisions, but, more mundanely, simply because no one thought about it.

There are all kinds of good goals—prolonging life, discovering scientific truths, becoming more efficient, and making a profit, to name just a few— and a sharp, well-intentioned focus on them can sometimes blind practitioners to the ethical implications of what is being done. It is hoped that a dose of ethical studies, focused on the activities involved, can serve as an antidote to this myopia.

2. To Prove There Is a Place in Business for Ethical Considerations

Another reason for studying ethics in the business context is to give the lie to the often-voiced view that ethics has no place in business because ethical considerations and business considerations are inherently in conflict. We might call the proponent of such a viewpoint a *business cynic*. (Note that this is not necessarily the same as saying "I don't care" about ethical considerations. The latter expresses an attitude and a certain kind of character, whereas the view that business and ethics inherently conflict may represent an intellectual belief.)

While I suspect that this viewpoint is more often expressed as an attempt to justify a particular instance or type of behavior than as a reasoned belief, it deserves to be dealt with nonetheless. It rests on mistaken notions about both ethics and business.

The mistaken perception of ethics could be summed up as the idea that "ethics must hurt." It is the belief that if an action is ethical, it must somehow be contrary to one's self-interest. This view, as we shall see in subsequent chapters, lacks foundation.

The notion that ethics and business are inherently incompatible also rests on a mistaken perception of business, which deserves to be addressed here. Usually this incorrect perception reflects some extreme belief about *profit*, namely that, to be profitable, a business must of necessity, act unethically.

> *The notion that ethics and business are inherently incompatible also rests on a mistaken perception of business. . .*

But to say that unethical behavior is *necessary* to achieve profitability is to make a claim about the way of the world. It wants proof, and proof, it would seem, is hard to come by. Look at all the profitable businesses. Are we to say that they all behave unethically? Certainly some do, but all? Moreover, even if we were to stipulate that not even one saintly company exists, that all have been unethical at one time or another, could the business cynic show that those ethical lapses were the key to profitability? Unlikely, to say the least.

Now if the business cynic wants to make the point that a business would have to act unethically to achieve *maximum profitability*, then, again, he or she would have to make a factual argument to support that case. However we define the term *maximum profitability*, the argument would at least have to show that, for *every* company, at some point the only way to increase profit would be to engage in some kind of unethical activity. It is hard to imagine how such an argument would go unless it were buttressed by unreasonable and unproven assumptions about the way the world works.

Besides, it is certainly not true that maximum profitability is the goal of every business enterprise. Of the many companies with mission statements that include a reference to profit, the term is frequently modified by qualifiers like *decent* and *fair*, and the achievement of profit is often constrained by goals relating to such things as *fair dealing, integrity*, and *good corporate citizenship*.

Finally, even if the relationship between ethical behavior and profit seeking could be shown to be problematic, that would concern just one aspect of ethical considerations in the business environment. While every business may seek to make a profit, in large organizations very few persons are directly or functionally involved with bottom-line decisions. Ideally it may be true that the performance of each division, department, section, and so on has a direct and discernible effect on a company's earnings; but the ethical issues encountered by many individuals—issues relating to harassment, corporate ladder-climbing, favoritism, cover-ups, etc.—are seldom framed in terms of profit and loss.

3. To Improve Business Ethics

Finally, there is the straightforward answer that the study of business ethics is needed because, all too often, the attempts to practice ethics while conducting business have not been very good.

This is not the same as the above statement that the ethical dimension of a given business situation may often be overlooked. Here we mean that, even when ethical considerations are given their due, the resulting actions or decisions are frequently short of satisfactory. The explanation that the people who make the decisions are bad, motivated only by self-interest, and so forth is simply not adequate.

> *. . . at work in our organizations and in the marketplace, we may find ourselves on unfamiliar ethical territory.*

Referring to the comments made at the beginning of this chapter, most of us are not ethical *naturals*, myself included. Whether innate or acquired, our disposition may generally guide us to do what is right, and we've probably had enough moral training that we know what we ought to do in everyday situations. But at work in our organizations and in the marketplace, we may find ourselves on unfamiliar ethical territory. We may feel opposite loyalties, sense conflicting obligations, and wonder where our duties lie. We've moved up to a new level, so to speak; the course we have to play is a little tougher. Some additional lessons and training could help us negotiate it a little better. That's where the study of business ethics comes in.

THINK ABOUT IT . . .

"In sports like hockey and football, you can do things to your opponent that are completely within the rules but that would be considered assault in the everyday world. It's the same in business. The rules from home don't apply. There aren't any rules. It's a jungle. Deal with it."

What do *you* think of this idea?

Wrap-Up Questions

1. With a limited budget, you are trying to make the most cost-effective decision for advertising an upscale home appliance. Your choice is between the *Herald* and the *News*. The *Herald* has larger circulation and reaches a higher-income demographic. The *Herald* is mainly bought at newsstands and other locations. On the other hand, the *News* is delivered to more homes, and it has a longer "table life" (i.e., it stays in the home longer). It costs 13 percent more to advertise in the *Herald*.

   Which statement is most correct?

   A. Having more facts would likely help in the decision-making process.
   B. If the facts were quite different, the decision would probably be different.
   C. Even if no more facts were available, the decision won't be arbitrary.
   D. All of the above.
   E. None of the above.

2. You must implement serious cost savings, but you also want to do the right thing. One of the alternatives available to you is to reduce wages across the board by cutting back on hours throughout the workforce. Another alternative is to achieve the same dollar savings by laying some people off. You know that 84 percent of your workforce consists of members of two-income families. You also know that the wages you pay are 8 percent above the median for comparable jobs. There is a general economic downturn in the region, and unemployment is high.

   Which statement is most correct?

   A. Having more facts would likely help in the decision-making process.
   B. If the facts were quite different, the decision would probably be different.
   C. Even if no more facts were available, the decision won't be arbitrary.

D. All of the above.

E. None of the above.

3. Josh thinks it is unfair that a new employee gets the same amount of vacation time as an "old-timer." "It's not fair," he says, "for everyone to receive the same amount of benefits when they haven't put in the same amount of work." Megan, on the other hand, thinks it is fair as long as everyone is treated equally. "We all get the same vacation time; we're all treated the same. It's fair."

Which statement is most correct?

A. Josh and Megan have a disagreement about the facts.

B. Josh and Megan are using "fair" in different ways.

C. Josh and Megan are both being arbitrary.

D. All of the above.

E. None of the above.

4. Which statement is most correct?

A. Through experience and training, a person can become better at business, but not at ethics.

B. Experience and training can't help make a person better at business, but they can help someone become better at ethics.

C. Experience and training can't help make a person better at business or ethics.

D. Through experience and training, a person can become better both at business and at ethics.

5. Which statement is most correct?

A. To make a profit, somewhere along the line you must be unethical.

B. If A makes more profit than B, then A must be more unethical than B.

C. Every company wants to make as much profit as possible.

D. All of the above.

E. None of the above.

6. Which statement is most correct?

A. It's OK to cheat in school, because school is competitive and the stakes are high.

B. It's OK to cheat in sports, because sports are competitive and the stakes are high.

C. It's OK to cheat in business, because business is competitive and the stakes are high.

D. All of the above.

E. None of the above.

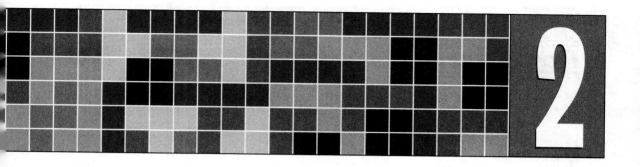

Values and Principles

PERFORMANCE GOALS

After completing this chapter, learners will be able to:

■ distinguish between values and principles.

■ indicate that all values are not equal and give examples.

■ discuss why people with the same values and/or principles might disagree.

■ discuss reasons for needing to rank or order values and give examples.

■ indicate whether values ever change and give examples.

■ describe how even the Golden Rule can lead to conflicts in its applications.

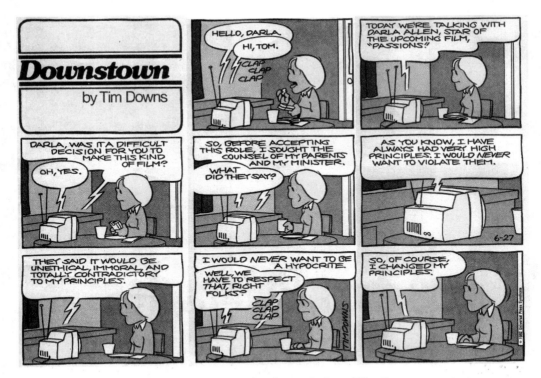

Copyright © 1982 by Tim Downs. Reprinted with permission of Tim Downs.

Warm-Up Questions

1. "When people have disagreements about ethical issues, it's always because they have different values."

    Agree   Disagree

2. Which things, if any, on the following list do you value?

sincerity	simplicity	diversity
honesty	efficiency	solitude
control	order	status
fairness	relationships	discipline

3. Pick one attribute from the list above, and for each of the others try to determine if you value them more than that one, less, or about the same.

4. "When values conflict, there can be no basis for resolving the conflict."

    Agree   Disagree

5. Which of the following do you believe to be correct about the Golden Rule? (No, not the rule that "the guy with the gold makes the rules.")

A. If everyone lived by the Golden Rule, there would be no conflicts.

B. If no one lived by the Golden Rule, there would be conflict all the time.

C. Some people practice the Golden Rule; others don't. Therefore, sometimes there's conflict and sometimes there's not.

D. The Golden Rule has nothing to do with conflict.

E. None of the above.

Much, if not most, of the talk about ethics is couched in terms of *values* and *principles*. We have all heard it said of people alleged to be grossly unethical that "they have no values" or "they have no principles." Commonly, when parties have a disagreement over a matter related to ethics, it is said that they have different values or that they are guided by different principles.

The language of *values* and *principles* presents one of those cases where the terminology is somewhat hazy. In everyday parlance, the terms are often used interchangeably and/or in ways that may overlap. Again we note that this does not generally present a problem. As long as there is no impediment to communication—and usually context makes matters clear—it is of little consequence that the terms are used without precise meaning.

In the sections that follow in this chapter, *values* and *principles* will be used in a manner that is consistent with their central meanings, but in a way that would *not* allow for them to be interchangeable. The purpose of this is so that we might clarify the relationships between certain concepts, regardless of how they are labeled. The aim of the discussion is to gain a better understanding of how moral rules and judgments come to be formed, not to advocate a special use of terminology.

VALUES

To value something is to "hold it dear." We value things that we seek out and attempt to maintain. Our values—the things that we value—may be objects, qualities, relationships, and states of affairs. For example, our values might include, respectively, *wildlife, beauty, friendship*, and *justice*. Not all values need be moral values.

Our values are revealed in our actions. What is it that we seek? What sorts of situations and relationships do we strive to create and maintain? In nonethical contexts our values may often be referred to as *priorities*. Thus, saying that an organization's priorities are revealed in its budget is another way of saying that we can discern the organization's values by seeing how it spends its money and where it makes its investments.

Values are sometimes characterized as either *intrinsic* or *instrumental*. Something that has intrinsic value is valued for itself. It is an *end in itself*. Instrumental value, on the other hand, means something is useful in achieving a goal. A thing has instrumental value because it serves as a *means to an end*. Tools like hammers and chisels have instrumental value. Their value resides in the fact that they are useful. Some have said that all human beings have intrinsic value and that, therefore, none of us should be treated as if we were of instrumental value only. In the 1960s this viewpoint was expressed in bumper stickers that said "Love people, use things."

> *Something that has intrinsic value is valued for itself. It is an end in itself.*

In recent years much has been made of so-called *family values*. Family values might include respect for parental authority, loyalty to the family unit, and time spent together. A full list would be considerably more extensive, and different proponents of family values would no doubt each have slightly different lists. Many of these values might be considered instrumental values, their worth based on the fact that they are a means to the end of maintaining family units. The family itself, however, might be held to have intrinsic value, to be valuable in its own right.

Alternatively, it could be held that the family unit itself is not intrinsically valuable, but that intact families have value because they contribute to overall social stability. Thus the preservation of the family, in this view, would be seen as instrumentally valuable to the achievement of a greater social end.

It is not the point here to conclude whether families have intrinsic or instrumental value. Rather we mean simply to show that what may have instrumental value in one society or person's scale of values may have intrinsic value in another.

> *. . . what may have instrumental value in one society or person's scale of values may have intrinsic value in another.*

Individuals, cultures, organizations, and businesses will generally have many values. Sometimes these values may conflict with each other when it comes to implementing them. This does not necessarily mean the values are contradictory or opposite. One can love both freedom and order. These are not inherently contradictory. A free society can freely choose to organize itself in an orderly manner. But there can be times when the two come into conflict.

An organization may value both efficiency of operations and the enhancement of employee creativity. Both might be perceived as having instrumental value toward the achievement of profit. Certainly there may be occasions when the attempt to implement these values would result in a conflict. In order to resolve the conflict, one value would have to be subordinated to the other, resulting in a ranking of values. "Values clarification" exercises, which involve posing conflicting-value situations, can yield sometimes surprising results, showing individuals or groups that—based on the choices they make—their hierarchy of values may be different than they had initially thought.

It would be a mistake to give the impression that the set of values held by an individual or an organization either is or ought to be somehow immutable and not subject to change. Those things that have instrumental value may be held in higher or lower esteem in different situations depending on their ability *in that situation* to help bring about a desired end.

If an organization values efficiency and employee creativity, it might do so because it perceives these values as helpful toward bringing about an ultimate result of profitability. They would be of instrumental value. In this scheme of things, profitability is the higher value.

Scenario

The FreeforAll Software company, hoping to enhance employee creativity, adopted a policy whereby all the company facilities were to be kept open 24 hours a day. Offices, so-called "village green" spaces, the cafeterias, even the recreational facilities would be open and available to all employees 24 × 7.

Not only did the policy accommodate the work habits of many employees who thrive on odd hours, but also it turned out to encourage the cross-fertilization of ideas from people in different areas who now were more likely to engage in conversations with fellow odd-hour employees in other parts of the company. You are more likely to converse with the stranger in the cafeteria at two o'clock in the morning than at noon with a hundred other people around, right?

Of course the new policy drove some of the efficiency-loving bean counters nuts. What a waste! Lights on and utilities running with nobody home. Some nights the cafeteria staff served only eight people (though there were other nights when they served 80). This, in their eyes, was a crazy way to run a business.

Suppose, on the one hand, that the policy described above yielded excellent results in terms of the employees' creative productivity—and that the ultimate bottom-line result was increased profits that far outweighed the increased costs of running the physical plant. In this case, enhanced creativity would trump the loss of efficiency, because it showed greater instrumental value toward bringing about a higher profit.

If, on the other hand, it turned out that the inefficiency resulted in losses greater than the bottom-line benefits gained from enhanced creativity, then the policy would presumably be modified or rescinded.

Efficiency and creativity might both be valued; but, in a particular situation, in this organization they would be rated according to their contribution to the higher value of profitability.

There is no question that one's hierarchy of values may change over time. Typically, as the years go by, *freedom* may take a backseat to *stability*, and *autonomy* may defer to *security*. This happens both in individuals and in organizations. The values driving a young start-up enterprise are quite likely to change as organizational maturity sets in. Yet, for both individuals and organizations, values are an important component of identity. Unless certain core values are retained, in an important sense neither the person nor the company can be said to be *the same*.

> ... for both individuals and organizations, values are an important component of identity.

It is a matter of ongoing debate whether values can be taught. Clearly, one can acquire a good deal of "head knowledge" about the values of a group, a company, or a culture without adopting the values as one's own. Knowing about values is not the same as holding them. Yet we must account for the fact that people do come to have values that at one time or another they did not have. Certainly training, albeit not necessarily formal, has something to do with this change. Positive and negative feedback play a role, as does teaching by example. There is truth to the adage that values are more *caught* than *taught*.

THINK ABOUT IT . . .

Do you value the same things now that you did 10, 20, or 30 years ago? If not, what has changed? Consider the same question about our country.

PRINCIPLES

Principles are the fundamental rules that implement our values. Thus if honesty is the value in question, its implementing principle could be stated as "Always be truthful" or, in its negative equivalent, "Never be untruthful."

> ... from the "Always be truthful" principle that implements the value of honesty, we might also develop more specific rules that would prohibit us from misleading anyone—even if no untruths are involved . . .

Principles are fundamental in the sense that other rules derive from them, but they do not themselves derive from any other rule. Other, more particular rules, for example, could follow from "Always be truthful." "Do not cheat" might be said to derive from the general principle to be truthful; and "Never claim the work of another as your own" might, in turn, derive from the "Do not cheat" rule. Similarly, from the "Always be truthful" principle that implements the value of honesty, we might also develop more specific rules that would prohibit us from misleading anyone—even if no untruths are involved—as we might also generate rules regarding promise keeping. All such derivative rules could be traced back to the general principle to tell the truth and its grounding value, honesty. But the general principle itself may not have been derived from some other rule.[1]

Principles are generally formulated as rules or imperatives (commands)— "Do this," "Don't do that"—and one of their features is that they are stated as *universals*. That is, they are not addressed only to certain persons, but they are meant for everyone. (However, if one does not adhere to the value that grounds the principle, one will not likely feel bound by it.) Moreover, principles are not held to be contingent upon any set of circumstances (e.g., "Tell the truth in situations where it will not cost you"), nor are they viewed as strategies for bringing about certain results ("If you want to be well thought of, tell the truth"). They stand *without qualification*.

Just as with values, though, it can pretty quickly be seen that principles or the rules generated from them can conflict in certain situations. When such conflict arises, then it will be necessary to rank one principle over the other. For example, loyalty to our friends and our organizations—including our companies—is an important value and may guide us to fall in line when an organization is challenged or questioned, and to protect our friends and not easily give them up. Yet we may also live by rules and principles that would have us minimize harm, obey the law, and be truth tellers. Now if we found ourselves in a position that many people were in during the past decade—knowing that our company, perhaps even our friends, had engaged in deceptions that were illegal and that would also probably cause harm to innocent persons—then we would have to decide what, if anything, we were going to do about it. And that decision would involve ranking our principles and values in order of importance.

It is tempting to think that there might be just one overarching ethical principle such that conflicts might never arise. Certainly one of the most frequently suggested candidates for an ultimate ethical principle is what is commonly called the Golden Rule, or one of its various formulations:

> *... one of the most frequently suggested candidates for an ultimate ethical principle is what is commonly called the Golden Rule ...*

> *Do unto others as you would have others do unto you.*

> *Treat people as you would want to be treated.*

> *Do not do things to other people that you would not want done to yourself.*

In one form or another this principle has appeared in major religions and ethical systems for thousands of years. It is not clear, however, that the Golden Rule in any of its formulations can provide a conflict-free guideline for making ethical decisions.

---

[1] Of course there may be systems of values and principles in which the principle of truth telling is indeed derived from some other rule. See the following remarks regarding the Golden Rule.

Frequently we find ourselves in situations where individuals or groups have competing interests and we must make a decision between them. When resources are scarce, conflicts arise. Some people have to be laid off in order to keep a company viable so that others might benefit. There are more qualified candidates than there are job openings. Competing suppliers both have an equally meritorious claim for your order, but only one can be selected.

Can the Golden Rule help us in such situations? Some would say "yes"—as long as everyone is treated fairly and judged or selected according to the same standards, then your action will be ethical, because that's the way you would want to be treated, isn't it? Maybe. Perhaps, though, some of us would want to be treated *preferentially*. If we are to treat others as we would want to be treated, then should we introduce those preferences into the process?

THINK ABOUT IT . . .

What value, or values, does the Golden Rule implement?

There are those who say that a rational person would prefer to be treated according to principles of justice so, therefore, it would follow that others should be treated according to principles of justice. But this is to prejudice the case. Some of us would rather be treated with mercy than justice, especially if we are honest about what we really deserve. Is this irrational? It doesn't seem to be. And, if it isn't, doesn't it follow according to the Golden Rule that we should treat others mercifully more than justly?

> *Because we can have sincere differences as to how we would want to be treated, we can have sincere differences as to how we think others should be treated.*

The Golden Rule is an ethical principle that enjoins us to treat others in the same manner we would prefer to be treated. Certainly it is generally a good rule to follow; but attempting to follow it does not mean that we can always avoid conflicting opinions. Because we can have sincere differences as to how *we* would want to be treated, we can have sincere differences as to how we think *others* should be treated.

THINK ABOUT IT . . .

An older worker with considerable seniority thinks that last-hired-first-fired is an equitable principle to apply during a round of layoffs, whereas a young new hire believes that performance and potential should be the principles for retention. Can the Golden Rule be helpful in devising an ethically sound policy?

VALUES, PRINCIPLES, AND ETHICAL DISAGREEMENTS

It should be clear by now that disagreement about the right course of action—what ought or ought not to be done—can occur among people who share the same values and principles. There may be sincere differences of opinion as to how the principle(s) in question ought to be applied; or there may be differences as to which among competing values is the higher or more important one.

> *. . . disagreement about the right course of action—what ought or ought not to be done—can occur among people who share the same values and principles.*

Not only can ethical differences arise from different interpretations or applications of the same principles, but contrary ethical conclusions can also result from different assessments of the empirical facts.

We are used to this in the day-to-day process of making business decisions. There's never enough information. And seldom is there unanimity in the assessments of the information we do have.

"How will the market react to this?"

"Is this ad campaign too edgy for our constituency?"

"Does our competition have the ability to meet this pricing?"

"Can this supplier continue to meet our needs?"

We may have honest disagreements about the correct answers to questions such as these, and our disagreements may lead to contrary conclusions and recommendations. But these differences are not traceable to different (business) principles. The differences stem from our dissimilar assessments of factual situations.

Many of our ethical quandaries and disagreements have the same character. Often they don't come about because of unclarity or disagreements about our values or principles; they arise because we are unsure or have differences of opinion about the facts of the case.

THINK ABOUT IT . . .

Some people believe that the use of so-called "recreational drugs" would be morally wrong even if it were legal. Others disagree, believing that there would be nothing morally wrong about using such drugs if they were made legal. Do you think these disagreements arise from different moral values, or from different assessments of the facts, or both?

TASTE, MANNERS, AND MORALS

It has been noted that not all values are moral values. Some people value solitude, while others do not. It is a matter of personal preference, more a question of taste than morality. The same can be said of principles. "Buy low and sell high" may be an excellent principle to follow; but no one would be inclined to characterize it as a *moral* principle. It does not present us with a moral duty. To willingly and intentionally violate this principle might be foolish, but it would not be morally wrong.[2]

Conversely, we can think of moral principles whose application could lead to norms of behavior that would have more to do with *custom* and *manners* than with issues of ethics and morality. Presumably none of us wants to be treated in a demanding, offensive, and boorish way. According to the Golden Rule, then, we ought not to treat others in such a fashion. But if we were to do so, our behavior would not, by most accounts, be considered immoral or unethical. It would just be bad manners. Consider the telemarketing practice of cold calling at and around the dinner hour. No one, we think, wants to receive such calls. So what about the practice of *making* such calls? It would seem to violate the Golden Rule. Is it immoral? That sounds a bit extreme, however else we might want to characterize the activity.

Is there a way to distinguish ethical principles and values from those that are merely matters of personal preference or cultural norms? Some have suggested that moral values are ones that are intrinsic, whereas nonmoral ones are instrumental. But this proposal seems inadequate; for, as has been noted earlier, a value that is only instrumental for one person might be intrinsic for someone else. *Orderliness*, some people may believe, is valuable in and of itself, and not because of anything it may provide a means to.

According to another approach, there is actually only one intrinsic value, and that is *pleasure*. All other values, it is said, are instrumental; they are valuable only because their realization produces pleasure. If moral values are intrinsic, it would follow then that the ultimate moral principle is to maximize pleasure. Its corollary would be to minimize pain.

The most common objection to this approach is that it, too, can lead to conflicting judgments inasmuch as there may be many varying opinions about what constitutes or produces pleasure. Moreover, most people would be reluctant to grant any positive moral status whatsoever to the pleasure that some deviant might experience from others' suffering.

From a practical point of view, it may suffice to acknowledge that issues of taste, cultural acceptance, manners, and morality form a continuum. Theoretically, we may not agree on precisely where to draw the lines between the various segments, but that matters little if, for the vast majority of cases, we know where we are.

We may encounter times when we have failed to consider the moral implications of what we do; but we usually don't have trouble recognizing

---

[2] One might imagine an extreme religion-like form of materialism in which the willful violation of the buy-low-sell-high maxim would have the status of a sin or a moral wrong; but this reveals more about the capacity of our imagination than it does about the moral matters of the real world.

them when they are pointed out. Our problems seldom have to do with whether or not we realize that a moral issue confronts us; they generally have to do with how we handle it.

THINK ABOUT IT . . .

The "Boy Scout Law" requires a Scout to be

■ Trustworthy	_____	■ Obedient	_____
■ Loyal	_____	■ Cheerful	_____
■ Helpful	_____	■ Thrifty	_____
■ Friendly	_____	■ Brave	_____
■ Courteous	_____	■ Clean	_____
■ Kind	_____	■ Reverent	_____

Are some of these moral values while others are nonmoral values reflective only of manners or taste? Try ranking them—there are 12—by assigning the highest numbers to the ones that most clearly have to do with moral values.

Wrap-Up Questions

1. A clothing retailer tells its salespeople to treat customers the way that they, the salespeople, would want to be treated. The company does this because they believe that it is good for business—customers will return more often, and they will tend to spend more.

   Which statement is most correct?

   A. This proves that business and morality don't conflict.

   B. This is an example of a nonmoral application of the Golden Rule.

   C. Company decisions are always driven by profit.

   D. All of the above.

   E. None of the above.

2. Connect the values with the company principles that are meant to implement those values.

Values	Principles
Fairness	Always use the best ingredients available.
Reliability	Always disclose any known material defects.
Honesty	Only take orders that you can fill.
Quality	Leads whose source cannot be traced will be handed out on a rotating basis.

3. If employee morale is important to a company for the reason that high morale leads to greater productivity, that would show that, in this case, employee morale has

A. instrumental value.

B. intrinsic value.

C. Both of the above.

D. Neither of the above.

4. Alan thinks that the company ad campaign is morally objectionable. All the ads feature attractive, younger people who are having a great time at some wonderful setting such as the beach or a ski resort. Alan believes this misleads consumers to think that if they use the product, then they too are going to be "beautiful people" who enjoy similar experiences.

David, on the other hand, doesn't think the ads are morally objectionable at all. He believes that they mislead no one and that no one thinks using the product would have that kind of effect on their lives.

Which statement is most correct?

A. David and Alan disagree about whether or not something is morally objectionable, hence they must have different values.

B. David and Alan disagree about whether or not the ad campaign is morally objectionable, but their disagreement is not based on different values.

C. A disagreement about what is or isn't morally objectionable can occur only between people who share the same values.

D. All of the above.

E. None of the above.

5. Which statement is correct?

A. A company's values may change, but an individual's values will remain constant.

B. A company's values may change, and so may those of an individual.

C. A company's values won't change, but those of an individual may change.

D. A company's values won't change, and neither will those of an individual.

6. There is a choice between awarding a bonus in one lump sum or spreading it out in payments over the year. Is it possible that different people, applying the Golden Rule, could come up with different decisions?

Yes   No

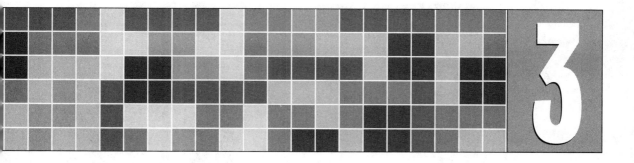

Sources of Influence

PERFORMANCE GOALS

After completing this chapter, learners will be able to:

- give examples of how cultures and sub-cultures influence standards and values.

- discuss whether law determines what is morally right or morally wrong, and discuss the relationship of law and morality.

- explain why professional and company codes are sometimes arbitrary or seem to be so.

- discuss religion as a source of moral standards.

- describe why religion-based morality is not always black and white.

*"Everybody's talking about ethics—find out what they are
and work some into our corporate image."*

Warm-Up Questions

1. We all get our *values* and our ideas of *right* and *wrong* from such different sources, there is little hope of ever having agreement on such matters.

    Agree   Disagree

2. Which phrase do you think would be the correct choice to make the following sentence true and complete?

"Religious people are (more likely than, less likely than, about as likely as) anyone else to see things as 'black and white' when it comes to assessing moral issues."

3. Do you agree or disagree with the following statements?

A. Our views about right and wrong are more strongly influenced by those who are close to us than by the larger culture.

        Agree   Disagree

B. Our views about right and wrong are more strongly influenced by the mass media than by those who are close to us.

        Agree   Disagree

C. Most people get their notions of right and wrong from the law.

Agree   Disagree

D. Only a few people get their notions of right and wrong from religion.

Agree   Disagree

E. In business matters, most people get their notions of right and wrong from company codes, rather than from the culture at large.

Agree   Disagree

4. With which of the following statements do you agree the most?

A. The moral values of our society have changed, and for the worse.
B. The moral values of our society have changed, and for the better.
C. The moral values of our society have changed, but they are neither better nor worse.
D. The moral values of our society haven't changed, but behavior has.
E. None of the above.

5. "Different cultures may have different values, but none is any better or worse than another."

Agree   Disagree

We get our ethical and moral codes, our sense of what is right and wrong, from a variety of disparate sources. Perhaps no two of us share the exact same influences in the exact same proportions. No wonder, then, that we occasionally have disagreements about such matters, and that we have conflicts both with other people and within ourselves. Conversely, because we share so many similar influences, it is not surprising that there is so much agreement among us.

Before examining some of the predominant influences on our ethical thinking, we must keep in mind that, ultimately, our ethical decisions are our own. Of course our thinking is influenced by sources outside of us; none

> . . . ultimately, our ethical decisions are our own.

of us would be expected to have invented our own version of morality out of whole cloth, so to speak. On the other hand, none of us is a moral automaton whose reactions and decisions are wholly determined by the sources and amounts of influence to which we have been exposed.

CULTURE

Much of what we learn of right and wrong, good and bad, we learn from those around us; and, in the modern world, the extension of "who is around us" has grown considerably. It includes not only people in our towns and

NON SEQUITUR © 1995 Wiley Miller. Dist. by Universal Press Syndicate. Reprinted with permission.

neighborhoods, but also—perhaps even more so—those who influence and those who are seen and portrayed in the various mass media, which include but are not limited to television, movies, popular music, and radio. Indeed, to some, the character of popular culture and the pervasiveness of its influence through the mass media are matters of despair. Be that as it may, we must acknowledge them.

We are also influenced in significant ways by smaller, closer subcultures. From street gangs to chess clubs, our society is composed of a vast number of subcultures formed around both vocations and avocations. These groups sometimes serve to reinforce the mores and standards of the wider culture, but on other occasions they may challenge and negate those standards. (In neither case is such influence necessarily either overt or intentional.) The influence of subcultures on the standards and attitudes of individuals within their respective spheres may be enormous.

The normative influence—the influence as to what should and should not be done—is frequently only implicit. Signs are not posted as to what is approved and what is not. Movies and TV shows do not carry subtitles saying "this behavior is OK" and "this behavior is bad." But they are no less powerful for that. What "everybody does" is something we are more likely to learn by observation and experience than by explicit instruction. And what is learned in this fashion is not easily forgotten or set aside.

Of course much of what we learn from our culture(s) has little or nothing to do with ethics; it is more a matter of taste, fashion, and manners. We learn what is cool, what is chic, what kind of attire is acceptable at work, and what sort of landscaping our neighbors expect us to maintain. None of these would count as moral issues. Our failure to conform to such often unwritten rules may cause life to be uncomfortable from time to time, and it can make our spouses displeased with us, but it doesn't result in moral condemnation. We can be nonconformists without being considered bad persons.

Some theorists have argued that moral standards are *wholly* determined by culture. According to this view, what is fashionable and what constitutes good and bad manners are determined by culture. Similarly, the theory goes, ethical right and wrong are also determined by the culture. Moreover, adherents of this position have joined it with the observation that cultures vary. They conclude therefore that, like many fashionable behaviors and manners, what is right or wrong, good or bad, and just or unjust can only be determined relative to a particular cultural setting. It is said that we can't, or shouldn't, ask in the abstract whether a given form of behavior is good or bad; we can only ask whether it is considered good or bad in a certain culture.

Certainly there are appealing and persuasive aspects to this kind of relativism. It helps explain and resolve the vexatious problems facing people who do international business and have to deal with bribery and other business practices that are considered acceptable in the home country and unacceptable in ours. It's a lot more comfortable to do what the Romans do when in Rome, if you are satisfied that there is no objective standard by which such behavior should be judged.

While tempting in certain circumstances, the idea that moral standards are determined by and relative to particular cultures is not easily believed if you think about it. For example, as mentioned earlier, some people in the United States deplore the immoral influence that the culture is imposing upon today's youth (and adults, for that matter). If we really believed that moral standards were culturally relative, then *that complaint wouldn't even make sense.* How could the culture—the alleged determiner and definer of moral standards—be accused of undermining moral standards? We don't have to agree with the moral views of the cultural critics, but we understand what they are saying. They are saying that there are standards of right and wrong that are independent of what is deemed acceptable by the culture. While we may disagree with the critics as to what those standards are and where they come from, we certainly see what point they are asserting.

THINK ABOUT IT . . .

What do you think are the predominant sources of cultural influence on people's values today? Rank them:

▪ Family	_____	▪ Movies & TV	_____
▪ School system	_____	▪ Government	_____
▪ Friends	_____	▪ Ethnic community	_____
▪ Church/religion	_____	▪ Other	_____

THE LAW

Many of our notions of what is right and wrong and good and bad are embodied in the law. Generally, we are influenced by the law not so much in the sense that we learn right and wrong from it as in the sense that what we have already learned is reinforced by it. The form of the law, insofar as it relates to behavior, is usually prohibitive. Certain kinds of actions are prohibited; few are encouraged.[1] Doing unjustified physical harm, stealing, discriminating, and harassing are all activities that most would agree are ethically wrong, and the law also prohibits them.

> *Generally, we are influenced by the law not so much in the sense that we learn . . . from it as in the sense that what we have already learned is reinforced by it.*

Although the law comes from the culture, its standards are certainly not equivalent to those prevalent in the culture at any given time. Sometimes the law lags behind culturally accepted notions of right and wrong. Laws that are "antiquated" in this way are sometimes repealed and often simply not enforced. There are other times when the law may represent what only a portion—not necessarily the majority—of the culture believes, and occasionally this causes serious and uncomfortable divisions. Differences of moral beliefs on issues ranging from drugs to abortion show us that the law itself cannot be a final arbiter of right and wrong. It can tell us what is legal and illegal, but that will not settle the moral issue.

While the injunction to obey the law may stand as a general ethical principle, few, if any, would hold it to be absolute. Laws, like the cultures from which they come, can embody ethical falsehoods as well as truths. They can be off the mark in this regard, and sometimes a higher ethical principle will require that they be disobeyed.

Conversely, though, there are occasions when the law may morally inform and educate. Consider discrimination and harassment. Over the years since laws prohibiting these behaviors have been enacted, one effect has been to enlighten and sensitize persons that these sorts of things are wrong, and that they would be wrong even if there were no laws prohibiting them.

Only a small portion of the law deals with behavior that, as it were, has an ethical dimension. Much of it has to do with process, structures, and procedures. Moreover, although there may be a general ethical rule that enjoins us to obey the law, the laws themselves do not necessarily identify behavior that in itself is unethical.

In California, it is against the law to drive more than 25 MPH in a school zone. Is it immoral (apart from the general injunction to obey the law) to drive

---

[1] Actually the tax laws provide some exceptions to this, where incentives are provided for undertaking various kinds of behavior. Generally this has little to do with ethically admirable behavior—buying a house or "banking" acreage may have little connection to inherent moral qualities. On the other hand, giving to charity, a morally positive thing to do, is definitely encouraged by our tax system.

26 MPH in a school zone? No. Illegal, yes; but not immoral. Suppose the limit were changed to 20 MPH. Then, with the new limit, it would be illegal to drive at 24 MPH, although not with the former (or the present-day) one. The speed limit change wouldn't make a previously morally acceptable act morally wrong.

In short, the law does not make what *was* morally acceptable into something that is now morally wrong. Nor, conversely, does the permission of a behavior by law confer upon it moral acceptability. Discrimination was morally wrong *before* the law prohibited it.

Many parts of the law relate to what is ethically right and wrong; but the law does not determine that. "Is it legal?" is a good question to ask of a policy or course of action, and a negative answer should give one pause. There are occasions when disobedience to a legal system may be the morally correct thing to do; but seldom do those situations have anything to do with business decisions or corporate policies. They are more typically conditions encountered by a reformer or a protester, not a CFO or sales manager.

Finally, a "yes" answer to the "Is it legal?" question can never be taken as sufficient to settle the ethical issue. "Yes, but is it right?" comes next.

THINK ABOUT IT . . .

Except in certain specific contexts, there is no law against lying. Why not? Should there be?

PROFESSIONAL AND ORGANIZATIONAL CODES

Many companies, organizations, and professional societies have codes of ethics, statements of values, or mission statements that include ethical directives. The ethical exhortations and prohibitions within such codes and statements are not, of course, the products of unique ethical values and principles. Rather they derive from general principles with which we are all probably familiar.

There are two chief values to professional and organizational codes. On the one hand, codes may reveal an ethical dimension to certain practices or industry-specific situations that we might otherwise never have realized. For example, the ethical code of the National Association of REALTORS® prohibits certain kinds of advertising practices—such as omitting the broker/company name in an ad—on the grounds that they are deceptive. Yet the idea that an ad without the company name might be deceptive probably would not occur to the typical agent.

Second, an ethical code that specifically addresses the kinds of circumstances peculiar to a vocation can, quite frankly, sometimes save us the time and trouble of having to work through the issues ourselves. While I would be the

> . . . an ethical code that specifically addresses the kinds of circumstances peculiar to a vocation can, quite frankly, sometimes save us the time and trouble of having to work through the issues ourselves.

last to advocate unthinking adherence to codes and directives, there is also little value in reinventing the wheel. Sometimes we do well, even in ethical matters, to give due respect to the thoughts and conclusions of those who have gone before us.

Frequently a company or professional ethics code will draw lines or impose requirements that may seem unduly strict. Conflict-of-interest prohibitions in the legal profession occasionally are taken to such extremes that one wonders if a firm would ultimately be able to represent only one client. Generally, professional codes tend to be overly cautious and to prohibit actions that might simply give the appearance or allow the potential of impropriety, even if no substantive wrongdoing is at issue.

An organization's ethical rules may sometimes seem arbitrary as well. A company might have an ethics rule prohibiting receiving from a supplier any gift whose value exceeds $50. One can understand how this might be considered arbitrary. The number might as well have been $55, or $45. This in turn may lead to creative attempts to circumvent the rule ("You *could* give me one $40 ticket to the same event on two different occasions . . . ").

That certain numbers or requirements in a code may be in some sense arbitrary is not an indictment of the code. The code's purpose is not in itself to be an ultimate arbiter of what is morally right and wrong. Part of the purpose of an ethics code is to provide people with rules that are easily understood and that generally help avoid (not eliminate) ethical problems. As with laws related to speed limits, this requires picking numbers and setting limits that could just as well have been slightly different.

> Part of the purpose of an ethics code is to provide people with rules that are easily understood and that generally help avoid (not eliminate) ethical problems.

Organizational and professional codes are equally likely to provide guidance and directives on matters that have little or nothing to do with morality. Sometimes the matters with which they deal (e.g., strictures having to do with advertising or with criticizing other members of the group) relate more to professional etiquette and "getting along" than to ethics. Indeed, some of the "getting along" provisions of professional codes have amounted to nothing more than price-fixing and anticompetitive agreements that have been determined as contrary to the public interest and illegal if not immoral.

As with the law, professional and organizational codes are a good place to look when assessing an action or policy; if the code prohibits it, or *seems* to prohibit it, take pause. Even though, as noted before, codes like these may contain elements that have an arbitrariness about them, the codes themselves do not tend to be arbitrary. They are generally the result of serious attempts to apply widely recognized ethical principles to the particular situations that occur within an industry or practice.

The other point to remember when dealing with professional and organizational codes is that one should be wary of falling into the same ethical fallacy we noted about the law. Just because something isn't prohibited by the code doesn't mean it is therefore an acceptable behavior or policy. We still have to ask, "Is it right?"

THINK ABOUT IT . . .

Does your company have an ethics code?

If it does, what parts would you say reflect general morality, what parts are industry-specific, and what, if any, are for "getting along"?

    If not, would it be useful to have one? If you were writing it, what would it say?

RELIGION

In this day and age, one might hesitate to bring the subject of religion into a discussion like this. Many people have no religious attachments at all. Others do, but theirs still differ from others' attachments. Must we consider all religions, only some, or only one? Even some religious people would say that religion is an entirely private matter and shouldn't be discussed at all.

"Well, actually, they are written in stone."

On the other hand, it would be totally naive to ignore the role that religion plays in the ethical thinking of many, many people. In a business setting, ethical decision making is quite likely to be a collaborative process. To be unaware of or to choose to ignore the fact that religiously influenced ethics may critically inform colleagues' or a constituency's thinking is to approach the task with less than a full set of tools.

Much can be made of the differences between religions as well as the differences within them. Frequently, though, these differences do not manifest themselves as disagreements about moral issues, but rather as quarrels about theological matters, liturgy, ceremonies, observances, and even dress. Actually, on matters related to central moral concepts such as honesty, justice, benevolence, and respect for life and individuals, there is probably more agreement than disagreement.

But where there are differences—be they about moral, theological, or even liturgical matters—they are liable to be expressed strongly and to be resistant to argument and change. Primarily this is because, for most religions, moral values and ethical directives have a god-given status that makes them inviolable. A person whose moral beliefs are not religiously conceived is more disposed to think that the beliefs might have flaws and to consider changing or reordering them.

Having said that, let me be quick to avoid misinterpretation. I don't mean to suggest that a person whose ethical values are not grounded in religion is therefore liable to be inconsistent, relativistic, and ready to change his or her standards on the slightest whim. Not at all. We have all known people of impeccable moral wisdom and integrity, steadfast in their principles throughout circumstances and over time, who had no religious attachments whatsoever.

> *... it would be a mistake to think that all whose morality finds its source in religion are therefore intransigent people ...*

By the same token, it would be a mistake to think that all whose morality finds its source in religion are therefore intransigent people who see the world of ethical choices as simply black and white, and who are insensitive to the needs and nuances underlying most moral dilemmas.

Indeed, some religion-based ethics have been at the opposite end of the spectrum from rigid, inflexible codes of behavior. Consider Rev. Joseph Fletcher, who may have been the most misunderstood Christian ethicist of the twentieth century. Fletcher was the chief proponent of a position known as *situation ethics*. He was as far removed from the stereotyped rigid religious ideologue as one can imagine. Yet neither was he the unprincipled relativist so often portrayed by critics of his viewpoint. Fletcher argued that the single guiding value of Jesus' ethics was *compassion*, and that the application of compassion often called for different judgments and different actions depending on the particulars of given situations. Certainly, this value did not lead to a strict adherence to rules.

Religions, of course, are part of our culture; and many of us have been influenced by religious beliefs and ethical views in ways and to an extent that we may not even imagine. If a proposed course of action seems to be at cross-purposes with a religiously based ethical concept, that may be a good reason to consider further. For the religious person, it may even be a conclusive reason for rejection.

THINK ABOUT IT. . .

Has it been your experience that religious people are generally more ethical, less ethical, or about the same as the rest of us? What explains this?

CONCLUSION

It is not my purpose to attempt to settle theories about the ultimate source of moral standards, the process by which they become known, and so on. Here we simply want to acknowledge that most of us acquire our values and ethical beliefs from a variety of sources. In many cases these sources overlap, and in some they conflict. Figure 3.1 represents this phenomenon to a certain degree, but it is not sufficiently complex to give a complete picture.

The reader is invited to improve the diagram and to reflect on its implications as it now stands. Are there some common standards that would call for all the circles to overlap at some point? Is there, as this diagram suggests, a portion of morals that cannot be attributed to *any* of these sources? Does this show that ethics are not objective? Be careful, for these are the kinds of questions that lead people into philosophy.

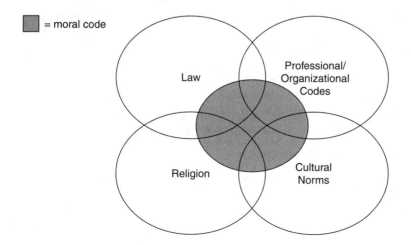

FIGURE 3.1   Overlapping sources of values and ethical beliefs.

Wrap-Up Questions

1. Which statement is most correct?

   A. Sometimes subcultures will be opposed to the values of the larger culture.

   B. Sometimes subcultures will be supportive of the values of the larger culture.

   C. Both of the above.

   D. Neither of the above.

2. The belief that society's moral standards are on the decline presupposes that

   A. cultural attitudes are the determiner of right and wrong.

   B. right and wrong are purely subjective, relative to each individual.

   C. religion is no longer influenced by the law.

   D. there are some standards of morality independent of prevailing cultural attitudes.

   E. All of the above.

   F. None of the above.

3. Different companies are liable to have different codes regarding accepting gifts. Some prohibit receiving gifts altogether. Some set a dollar-value limit. Others only offer guidelines. The fact that these differences exist shows that company ethical codes have no basis in general morality.

   True   False

4. Which of the following statements is true?

   A. Some laws have nothing to do with morality.

   B. If something is immoral, then it is also prohibited by law.

   C. Usually, we learn moral right and wrong from the law.

   D. All of the above.

   E. None of the above.

5. Even if people belong to different religions, you can count on the fact that they will hold the same beliefs about what is right and what is wrong, and that they will have no flexibility on those points.

   True   False

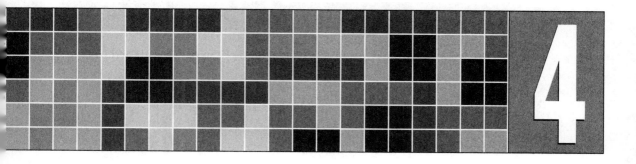

Ethical Judgments

PERFORMANCE GOALS

After completing this chapter, learners will be able to:

- list three factors to consider when looking at consequences as a basis for ethical evaluation of action.

- indicate whether individuals can estimate the results of their actions.

- compare focusing on results with focusing on intent.

- discuss the position that all actions are motivated by self-interest.

- name at least two difficulties with focusing on rules.

Warm-Up Questions

1. "It is virtually impossible to predict the consequences of our actions."

    Agree   Disagree

2. Which of the following statements do you think is correct?

    A. Sometimes even the best business decision will have a downside, but that doesn't happen with ethical decisions.

    B. Sometimes even the best business decision and the best ethical decision will have a downside.

    C. If anyone truly makes the best decision possible—whether a business decision or an ethical decision—there will be no downside.

    D. None of the above.

3. "Last quarter more than 150 companies gave to relief efforts for disaster victims. Now, that may be nice for the victims, but no one should give any moral medals to the companies. Anytime a company does something, there's always something in it for them. They always act out of self-interest."

    Agree   Disagree

4. "Any company that wants ethical behavior from its employees should have a published set of rules to follow so that employees would never have any doubt about what is the right thing to do."

    Agree   Disagree

5. Even though the law did not require it, Johnson & Johnson recalled the product Tylenol when it was learned that there had been disastrous cases of tampering. In order to know whether Johnson & Johnson did the ethically right thing, we would need to know

    A. the results of their action.

    B. their motives.

    C. whether what they did was required by moral rules.

    D. all of the above.

    E. none of the above.

When we talk about making ethical judgments, no one should get upset that we are being *judgmental* or that we are setting ourselves up as somehow superior to others. If we are to be able to talk about what we should and should not do, what is preferable and what is to be avoided, then we are going to have to make judgments. We must be able to evaluate behavior—especially our own—and to do so, we must apply criteria that result in a judgment. Let us not shrink from this task.

There are generally three different bases for evaluating actions as right or wrong, good or bad. One basis is to look at the *consequences* of the action; another basis for evaluation resides in looking to the *agent*, the person or entity who chooses and initiates the action, and examining the *motives* or *intentions* involved; and, finally, another basis for evaluation consists in isolating the *qualities of the act itself*, independent of the agent and the results.

CONSEQUENCES/RESULTS

In the discussion that follows, we will use the terms *consequence* and *result* interchangeably.

Consequence- or results-oriented ethics maintains that when we are seeking to know which among various alternatives to choose, the only ethically relevant question to ask is, "What will the results be?" According to this view, it is the results of what we do that make an action good or bad. "Never mind codes, and never mind what anyone may think; the right thing to do is that which will produce the best results."

This statement is incomplete, though, for the adequacy of results-oriented ethics depends on a fuller explication of the concepts of *results* and *good results*. Without such further consideration, results-oriented ethics becomes a straw man, easily dismissed. Whether it was ever true that what was good for General Motors was good for America, *good* in the ethical sense can never be understood as simply meaning good for this company or that.

Those who locate the ethical quality of an act or policy in its consequences will address three issues: (1) the people affected by the results, (2) the kind of results, and (3) the long-term effects.

Whether or not a course of action is the right thing to do doesn't depend only on its consequences for a special group, a favored few. We must consider the results for *all parties who will be affected*. A business decision may have consequences for a variety of constituencies as it were. Many companies have recognized that decisions to relocate facilities don't just impact employees and shareholders. They may affect community members, suppliers, local businesses, and public facilities, to name just a few. All such parties can be held to be *stakeholders* in the decision, and its effects on them are relevant toward determining the decision's ethical character.

> *... those who would test actions by their consequences also must look to the long-term effects of an action.*

Another issue to be addressed by those who focus on results is the *kind* of results that are being considered. It is too easy, and mistaken, only to compute dollars-and-cents outcomes. We have to ask more generally, albeit vaguely, "What is the potential for this action to produce happiness or well-being, and, conversely, what is the likelihood that it will cause pain (of any kind) or unhappiness?"

Finally, those who would test actions by their consequences also must look to the long-term effects of an action. It does not suffice to know that, in the short run, results will be good and the well-being of all affected will be increased; we also have to think about long-term consequences. There is no ethical or business award for a decision that produces profits, employment, and community goodwill in the short term if the long-term results are groundwater pollution, widespread illness, and class-action lawsuits.

Not surprisingly, a number of objections have been raised to the idea that the ethical evaluation of actions should be based on consequences. The objections are both practical and theoretical.

A simple practical objection to the results-oriented view is that it is too hard to apply. The objection might go something like this: "It's hard enough to determine the overall and long-term effects of an action after it has taken place, but it's harder still—frankly impossible—to know these things *before* we act. We want to do the right thing, but how can we know what the right thing is if it takes a comprehensive crystal ball to make the assessment?"

A more theoretical objection to a consequence-based ethic is that it simply fails to take into proper account other basic ethical notions such as justice and loyalty. Considering everyone who is affected, without allowing anyone to have "special status," ignores the fact that some parties have, so to speak, moral claims on us. We can sympathize with, even admire, the employer who says that the effects a decision has on employees are of greater concern than the effects on strangers.

There are counters to these objections, and counters to the counters, but to engage them would be to go beyond our purpose. Let us simply conclude this section with two observations in support of the view that ethical judgments should be based on consequences.

The first is that evaluating on the basis of consequences is something we do all the time, in business, in ethical contexts, and in everyday life. Of course there may be truth to the theoretical argument that we can't with absolute certainty know what the results of our behavior will be; but, as a matter of fact, we often make such assessments, and more often than not we are right, or at least right enough for the purposes at hand.

Second, one attractive feature of results-oriented ethics is that it allows us to consider and compare alternatives. We can weigh different options by their expected consequences and arrive at one alternative that is "more right"—or "less worse"—than another, without having to get into simplistic categorizations of either *good* or *bad.*

THINK ABOUT IT . . .

We frequently evaluate business decisions on the basis of their results. Is there any reason not to judge ethical decisions on the same basis?

INTENTIONS AND MOTIVES

A second view regarding ethical judgments proposes that our evaluations should focus on the *intentions* of the agent—individual or corporate—who initiates the action. Advocates of focusing on intentions point out that once a person does something the results are out of his or her control; and, for that reason, they say, it is not appropriate to base moral judgments on consequences. No doubt there is a good point to this.

We noted in the previous section that the world isn't random. Most things we do turn out to have roughly the effects that we intended. Were it otherwise, we couldn't begin to know how to behave, at the most rudimentary level. Still, and especially when we are dealing with complex issues, events occasionally have a way of getting away from us. The best-laid plans can go awry, and it seems inappropriate that ethical judgments should always be made on the basis of that which so often is beyond our control.

Added to these observations is a related concern raised in the preceding section—that frequently (theoretically, always) it is even harder either to anticipate or to discover all the *long-term* results of what we do. The ripples on the pond extend far beyond our observation. We can't completely know *who* has been affected by our acts, nor *how* they have been affected.

Thus, it is concluded, in order to judge an action we need to look to the agent. What was he or she *trying* to accomplish, and why? Did the person act out of pure self-interest with no regard to others, was the behavior generously motivated, or was it somewhere in between? These, it is said, are the relevant kinds of questions to ask, regardless of how things actually turned out.

> *. . . in order to judge an action we need to look to the agent. What was he or she* trying *to accomplish, and why?*

Even if we agree that intention and motive are the key, if not the only relevant factors in making ethical judgments, there is still room for differing opinions as to which motives are the "right" ones. One suggestion has been to use an intention-oriented version of the results test suggested in the preceding section. From this perspective, the key to right action would be that one acted with *the intent to achieve results that would maximize the well-being of all who are affected.* This still puts emphasis on the importance of results, but lets the agent "off the hook" for that which is beyond his or her control.

Others, who might be considered more rule-oriented, would contend that the relevant issue concerns the agent's perception of *duty*, or what he or she was supposed to do. Good intent, it might be said, does not simply consist in trying to bring about good results. Good intent involves trying to do what moral duty requires, and that is not, or not merely, trying to bring about good results.

Thus, someone who holds the Golden Rule as the supreme moral principle might argue that a person acts rightly if his or her intent is to implement the Golden Rule: as long as the motive of the act is to treat others as you would be treated, you have done the right thing.

A person whose ethics derive from religious belief might say the same sort of thing, only specifying that the motivation of the action must be to implement the moral rules or commands of that particular religion. If one's intention is to conform to the moral duties imposed by one's religion, then, according to this view, one acts rightly.

Certainly there is much about intention-focused views that has appeal. Yet there are difficulties as well. One problem is that an action may be right at one time yet not so at another, depending not on the circumstances but on the agent's motive. This makes ethics somewhat difficult to teach, especially when so much is taught by example.

There are also theoretical objections. One has to do with the inaccessibility of other persons' inner states. Seldom, if ever, it might be argued, do we know someone's intentions or real motives. But this would mean that we are never or hardly ever able to make moral judgments about actions. From this perspective, an ethical view that is so inapplicable is not worthy of consideration.

Finally, there are those who would argue that all of our motives are the same, i.e., the furtherance of self-interest. If that view were correct, then it would be pointless—or impossible—to judge actions on the basis of intentions because, ultimately, all intentions would be the same.

Self Interest

The claim that all actions—individual or corporate—are based on self interest is a serious and far-reaching position. It merits examination in detail. (For ease of reference, let us call this the Self-Interest view.)

First, let us acknowledge the appeal of the Self-Interest position. That is, it plays on the correct observation that many acts claiming to be "selfless" or "done for the sake of others" are actually motivated by self interest. Whether we are talking about charitable giving, environmental beneficence, or simple acts of (apparent) kindness, we all can think of examples where the motive behind the action had to do with the furtherance of some self interest.

But to acknowledge this does not mean we accept the all-encompassing claim of Self Interest. Sure, we will concede that many actions are motivated by Self Interest—even many that are not described as such—but, *all*? Here, we want proof.

The proponent of the Self-Interest theory must deal with two kinds of counterexamples: (1) the well-known, widely reputed examples of people who have acted, as one says, "selflessly," and (2) our personal, self-reported examples.

In the first category, there is the Mother Teresa (or pick your favorite saint and/or noble character) example. Here we have a person who seems to epitomize selflessness, who lived her life doing things for others. How can the proponent of the Self-Interest theory convince us that our assessment of her is mistaken?

1. He or she might say, "Well, that is what she wanted to do." But, saying this does not establish that she acted out of self interest. She may have *wanted* to do things that were decidedly *not* in her self interest. The Self-Interest response here is inadequate because "I want to do X" is not equivalent to "I believe X is in my self interest."

2. Second, the supporter of the Self-Interest view might say, "Doing the things she did actually was rewarding to her. She gained great satisfaction from doing them." But this doesn't establish the Self-Interest position either. For one thing, the fact that she received satisfaction from tending to the ill and the poor doesn't prove that receiving satisfaction was the *reason* for her doing so. Receiving satisfaction may have been a result of what she did, but it may have merely been an incidental result. (When we talk, we redistribute air molecules in the room. That is a result of talking, but it is not our reason for talking).

3. Finally, the supporter of the Self-Interest position might say, "A person like Mother Teresa may *appear* to be acting for the interests of others, but actually she is 'storing up her reward in heaven.' She does what she does in order to receive what she believes is her future reward."

   By this we are supposed to believe that the behavior of the person in question is actually motivated by a hidden agenda, that there is some self-interest calculator at work. But note that no proof is available for such a claim. It is just stated as a given, assuming what needs to be proved. In logic, that is called "begging the question."

The second category of counterexample with which the self-interest proponent must deal concerns the self-reported acts not based on self-interest. (It is acknowledged that perhaps not everybody can offer such a counterexample.) Here, one might say something like, "Look, my spouse (lover, partner, friend) wants me to rub his neck, so I do. I *might* be doing that because I believe it will ultimately result in some benefit to me—and sometimes that might even be my reason for doing it—but that's not necessarily why I do it. Sometimes I just do it for his benefit."

The three objections listed for the first category, above, can all be raised here, and they can all be similarly dismissed. But, in this category, the proponent of the self-interest view must also say something else, namely, "You *thought* you weren't acting for reasons of self-interest, but *actually* you were." Here, the self-interest view is having to claim its correctness over our own self-awareness. But why should we accept that? Again, it seems to *assume* what needs to be proved.

RULES AND PRINCIPLES

We have considered basing ethical judgments on the results of actions and on the intentions that underlie actions; perhaps there is some way to consider *actions themselves*, abstracted both from their results and the agents.

One suggestion along this line is that an action can be considered a right action *if it conforms to or is subsumed under a set of moral rules.* Simply put, if it conforms to the rules, it is the right thing to do; if it conflicts with them, it is wrong. The simplicity and straightforwardness of such a view are appealing, but the debate begins when we ask "Which rules?"

Almost everyone is exposed at a young age to a simple and straightforward set of moral rules: "Don't tell a lie," "Don't steal," "Keep your promises," and so forth. Introducing rules is an early form of moral teaching, as it is a means of establishing acceptable behavior, both moral and nonmoral. At some early point, "Wash your hands before dinner" and "Put away your toys" are likely to loom as large as the injunction to be truthful.

One of the problems of equating *right action* with *acting according to the rules* is that we too frequently encounter situations that the rules do not specifically address. We may not know how or if the rules apply. Such situations may lead to the generation of more rules; but the only way new rules can come about is by applying the principle(s) from which the original rule(s) are derived.

The Golden Rule, for example, can be seen as a general moral principle that underlies a variety of specific moral rules. Prohibitions against lying, stealing, promise breaking, and so on can be seen as derived from the general rule that you ought not to treat people in ways that you do not want to be treated.

Thus by expanding the view that links the ethical qualities of acts to particular rules, we might arrive at a view that an act is right if it conforms to certain principles, namely the principles that underlie the rules. A version of this relates to the Golden Rule: an act can be said to be right only if you would want to see everyone behave that way. In other words, it can't be right just for you but not for everybody else.

This is abstract; it is not a question of what someone's intention is or was. If we want to know if it is morally acceptable for someone to lie on a particular occasion, the question would not be, "What is the person's intention?" nor would it be "What will be the overall results of lying?" Rather, we would have to ask ourselves if we find it acceptable for everyone to lie.

"For everyone to lie on *every* occasion" is the more or less traditional version of this view. A more relevant version would probably be to consider this question: "Would you find it acceptable for everyone to lie *in this type of situation* [where you describe the relevant features of the situation]?"

This approach, stated in a more negative formulation, is a familiar line of moral argument, the one which asks, "What if everyone did that?" The point, we all know, is that *if it would not be acceptable or desirable for everyone to act in such a fashion, then it presumably wouldn't be acceptable for a particular individual to act in that way either.*[1]

It is here that we begin to get a flavor of the basic moral precept that what applies to one, applies to all, and vice versa. No one has special status.

Many of the people inclined to focus on consequences find, nonetheless, that there are practical reasons for basing ethical evaluations on the *principles* of actions, rather than on their actual results. While it may be acknowledged that results are frequently uncertain and difficult to calculate in particular cases, it can still be said that we know in general what sorts of consequences are liable to follow from various classes of actions.

> *. . . we begin to get a flavor of the basic moral precept that what applies to one, applies to all, and vice versa.*

We have good reason to think that, generally speaking, more overall harm than benefit comes from dishonesty, deceitfulness, and the like. Hence, it is advocated, we may adopt rules and judge actions according to conformity with those rules, based on what *in general* would be the results of the acts in question. Thus, from this perspective, we could say of a particular case that it would be wrong to steal, even if we didn't know what the actual overall long-term consequences of stealing would be in that actual situation.

Looking at it this way, rules are viewed as "rules of thumb." "Red sky in the morning, sailor take warning." "Pass on third down and long yardage." "Buy the least expensive house in a nice neighborhood." These rules don't always work, but if followed, they will generally produce the desired results. Moreover, *even if a particular application doesn't yield the desired ends, to have followed the rule will have been to do the right thing.* Just as some have said, "No one was ever fired for buying IBM," a person who took the principles-based position would say, "No one will be condemned for telling the truth."

This approach has a number of attractive features. While concerned with results, it still provides us with a framework of rules—ethical rules of thumb, if you will—that relieve us from engaging in the too-often hopeless task of trying to figure out all the potential effects of particular decisions. Moreover, this point of view allows us to account for the experiences that we have all had—in everyday life as well as in ethical situations—where we *just know* the right thing was done, even though results didn't turn out the way they were supposed to.

---

[1] Here, though, we see the apparent weakness of describing actions too specifically. "Of course it is morally wrong to pad your expense account. What if everyone did that?" "Well," the cynic (or realist) might reply, "as a matter of fact everyone *does* do that. The results are tolerable enough, so maybe it's not so bad." In this case the moralist may believe it is more relevant to describe the activity *generally* as a form of stealing which, presumably, no one could want everyone to do in all situations.

THINK ABOUT IT . . .

We've all heard, "Rules were made to be broken." Just what does this statement mean? Can you give an example? Is it true in business? In ethics?

CONCLUSION

Rather than debating which of the above approaches to ethical evaluation is *the* right one, we might more profitably conclude that each has its place. Sometimes focusing on results is the most appropriate method. Sometimes looking to a person's intentions works best. And, sometimes, we will want to refer to rules and duties.

Despite the theoretical objections about our inability to know all relevant results, as a matter of fact, every day in all sorts of circumstances, we make decisions based on estimates of what will happen. We couldn't function in the world unless we did, and our general success in getting along shows that the task is far from impossible.

It is important to recognize our ability to estimate and calculate results, not because we need to do so in *every* ethical situation that confronts us, but because we need to do so in some of them. Having rules to follow is also both useful and desirable. This is true in ethics no less than in the world of practical experience. We don't need to keep reinventing the wheel. But sometimes the rules conflict, and sometimes we are not sure how to interpret them. Sometimes following them will be clearly at odds with what would yield morally preferable results. In such times we may have to prioritize, or to decide based on what we perceive the results will be.

Finally, there is a time and a place for looking at intentions and motives as well. While most of the time intent and results go hand in hand and motive is clearly discernible in action, we still want to be able to distinguish the two in special cases. There is the well-meaning falsehood that may be intended to heal, not to harm; and there is the well-intended act that may go awry. Conversely, and oddly enough, malevolent motives can sometimes result in beneficial consequences. The law commonly seeks to distinguish among motives, and so should we. We neither want to condemn the good-hearted bungler who fails to achieve the good that he intends, nor do we want to praise the scoundrel who would appear to be a saint.

Wrap-Up Questions

1. Although faced with severe business problems, the directors of the ABC Company voted to pay bonuses to its key executives. In part, this was done as an incentive to keep the executives from jumping ship. It was felt that it would be inadvisable to make the bonus decision public at this time, even though it was bound to be learned at a later date.

   Shortly thereafter, the company won a major package of wage and benefit concessions from its employees. Employees felt this was preferable to going through what appeared to be an imminent bankruptcy.

   Later, at the time of the S.E.C. filing, news of the bonuses produced a tremendous backlash. The employee groups reneged on their concessions, saying they had been obtained under false pretenses; a significant consumer boycott was mounted, and ABC stock plummeted.

   Which statement seems most correct?

   A. The directors did not pay sufficient attention to the long-term consequences of their action.

   B. The directors did not pay sufficient attention to the interests of all the stakeholders.

   C. The directors may have meant to act in the best interests of the company.

   D. There is no apparent reason to think that the directors acted out of self-interest.

   E. All of the above.

   F. None of the above.

2. "If we lay off 10 percent of our people now, it will certainly cause a great deal of hardship. The economy is down, and they are not likely to find other jobs. On the other hand, if we try to hang on as we are, and we keep hemorrhaging cash, we may have to let 20 percent go in the spring. We could try cutting back on everyone's hours, but I don't think that can effect enough of a savings to matter."

   This illustrates the notion that

   A. there is always a right or wrong choice.
   B. motive is what counts.
   C. we can always find a rule to show us the right thing to do.
   D. sometimes the best choice may be the "least worst" alternative.

3. The awards program that Jordan devised was supposed to build incentive and camaraderie in the sales team. Instead, it resulted in resentment, divisiveness, and jealousy.

   This is an example of a case where we might want to distinguish intentions from

   A. results.
   B. rules.
   C. stakeholders.
   D. self-interest.

4. "Regardless of the good consequences for consumers, Johnson & Johnson must have figured out a benefit to the company from its Tylenol decision. We know this, because we know that all actions—be they of a corporation or an individual—are based on self-interest."

   Can this viewpoint be proven? Yes   No

5. Mary Lynne, in procurement, found an incredible way to "beat the system" and to charge all sorts of personal purchases to the company in a manner that could never be traced. Her co-worker, Erik, was very disturbed by this and sought to convince her not to continue. In the course of their discussion, he appealed to her by saying, "What if everyone did this?"

   In saying this, it was Erik's intention to

   A. call Mary Lynne's attention to the consequences of her behavior.
   B. point out to her that many others might follow her example.
   C. appeal to the notion that, if it would be bad for everyone to do something, it wouldn't be right for one person to do it.
   D. appeal to the notion that if one person shouldn't do something, no one else should do it.
   E. All of the above.
   F. None of the above.

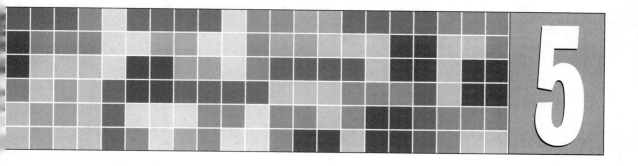

Justification, Rationalization, and the Analysis of Moral Choices

PERFORMANCE GOALS

After completing this chapter, learners will be able to:

- distinguish justification from rationalization.

- identify and describe at least two forms of justification.

- indicate why unequal results do not necessarily imply unequal or unfair treatment.

- describe two levels of questions regarding justice or fairness.

- describe a useful test of the fairness of a set of rules.

- discuss how rationalizing differs from making excuses.

Warm-Up Questions

1. "We always want to avoid the philosophy that the ends can justify the means."

   Agree   Disagree

2. Which statement do you think is most correct?

   A. A system can't be justified if people receive unequal rewards and benefits.

   B. A just system is one that will distribute benefits equally.

   C. A policy is fair only if everyone is treated according to the rules.

   D. All of the above.

   E. None of the above.

3. Which statement do you think is most correct?

   A. Some companies treat everyone according to the rules, but the rules really aren't fair.

   B. Some companies treat everyone according to the rules, and the rules are fair.

    C. Some companies have fair rules, but they don't treat everyone according to the rules.

    D. Some companies have unfair rules, and they don't treat everyone according to the rules.

    E. All of the above.

    F. None of the above.

4. "Rationalizing behavior is the same as justifying it."

    Agree   Disagree

5. "I know I shouldn't have used the company credit card then. I was desperate. My own card was maxed out, and I promised my wife I would get those tickets. I'll never do it again."

This is an example of

A. justification.

B. rationalization.

C. excuse.

D. all of the above.

E. none of the above.

We can see a variety of ethical concepts at work when we look at the process of *justification.*[1] When we are called upon to justify an action, we are called upon to explain it, to analyze why this action was chosen rather than some other. But what is asked for is not an explanation in the causal sense. We are not, for example, being asked for a psychological analysis. Rather, we are being asked to show why what *was* done is what *ought* to have been done. We need to show why the choice was ethically preferable to some alternative. The explanation that is asked for is a moral explanation.

JUSTIFICATION AND PRIMA FACIE WRONGDOING

Not every action requires justification. It would be odd to ask someone to justify having done something that was plainly a good thing to do. The question of justification only arises when things seem to be amiss.

When we say that something has a prima facie characteristic, we mean that it *apparently* has such a characteristic. In a legal context, to say that a plaintiff has a prima facie case means that, on initial inspection at least, there seems to be something to it; but it is still possible that further analysis may require the judgment to be revised.

---

[1] It should be clear that we are here restricting our discussion to the notion of *justification* as it is used in ethical discourse. Of course there are all sorts of uses of *justification* in nonethical contexts. We may be asked to justify a budget request, or we might be asked to justify the selection of a particular supplier. The process is similar to the process of justification in ethical contexts, but not exactly the same.

In justifying a course of action in ethics, what might appear prima facie to be wrong may, upon appropriate examination, be shown to be right or acceptable. Because lying is generally wrong, any instance of lying would appear to be prima facie a case of wrongdoing. However, a close examination of some particular case might show that the lie helped prevent great harm and was therefore justified.

Implicit in the notion of justification is the idea that some moral rules may be more important than others, or, to put it another way, that some values may be higher than others. A person who values life above honesty would have no difficulty justifying lying if it were necessary to save a life.

> Implicit in the notion of justification is the idea that some moral rules may be more important than others . . .

If a person believed that all moral rules had equal status, then no reason could ever justify breaking any of them. Any violation would be equally wrong, with no one outweighing the other. Such a view would be extreme to say the least. A more likely view holds that some, but not all rules are inviolable, and that only some values cannot be subordinated to any others.

The idea of justification shows that doing the right thing doesn't always involve clear and easy choices. Sometimes our alternatives are all flawed in one way or another. We choose the best (or the least worst) alternative available, even though it may involve doing something that is prima facie wrong; and we justify that choice by showing that any other alternative would have involved even greater wrong. In this respect we once again see that making ethical decisions can be like making business decisions. Very seldom are we presented with a perfect alternative. All options may have a downside. Often we must settle for choosing that which appears to be the least worst.

THINK ABOUT IT . . .

Can you recall a business decision that had a definite business downside but that was justified because of some greater business benefit that it produced?

ENDS AND MEANS

Earlier we referred to the idea of certain things being *ends in themselves*. Here we want to focus on the concept of *ends* as *results*. To ask what our end is involves asking what results we are trying to bring about, what we are attempting to achieve.

Now all of us have heard at one time or another that "the ends don't justify the means." Indeed, sometimes a point of view is considered to be conclusively refuted if it can be shown or said that the view in question represents an ends-justify-the-means philosophy. The position that ends can never justify means bears some careful examination.

If the ends are the results, what are the *means?* The means refer to the methods by which the results are brought about. They are the activities that lead to the results. To say that "the ends cannot justify the means," then, would be to assert two things:

■ First, this statement suggests that there is something *wrong* with the means, that the activity employed to bring about a certain result is at least prima facie wrong. (If the means weren't wrong, the question of justifying them wouldn't even arise.)

■ Second, this statement claims that the end, the result in question, is not good enough to outweigh the wrong attached to the means. *If the value represented by the results is not higher than the value violated by the activity, then the ends will not justify the means.*

But once this is all clearly understood, then we can see that there is little to recommend the view that ends can *never* justify means. Think about it. In the process of justification, we show that something that *appeared* to be the wrong thing to do really wasn't. One of the ways we prove this is by showing that the results of an action outweighed (on the value scale) the negative aspect(s) of the action itself. For example, as noted earlier, an instance of lying might be justified by showing that *in that particular circumstance* the lying prevented a great harm that would have resulted from telling the truth.

To say that the ends *never* justify the means would be to make the implausible claim that there are never situations when the ethically positive aspects of some result will outweigh the ethically negative aspects of the activity that produced it. That claim is much too general and unsupported. Ethics requires more careful thinking than this.

> *To say that the ends never justify the means would be to make the implausible claim that there are never situations when the ethically positive aspects of some result will outweigh the ethically negative aspects of the activity that produced it.*

The more plausible, albeit weaker, claim is still relevant: "Often, the ends do not justify the means," or more colloquially perhaps, "Not every end will do." This assertion is supported by a variety of circumstances.

Frequently people seek to justify their prima facie wrong behavior by appealing to their own self-interest. Generally, this will *explain* why they did what they did, but it won't suffice to justify it. "I lied about my expenses in order to fatten my own wallet" doesn't really pass moral muster.[2]

Even ends that encompass the well-being of others, i.e., that extend beyond simple self-interest, may not be sufficient to justify employing prima facie wrong means. Cheating is not justified on the grounds that it would

---

[2] It should not be inferred from this that there is anything inherently ethically wrong about acting in one's own self-interest. The point is only that in many instances the end of self-interest will not be sufficient to justify having done something that is prima facie wrong. Self-interest is further discussed in Chapter 4, pp. 44–45, and Chapter 7, p. 83.

enable victory, even if the winning would result in great happiness for many people, perhaps even more people than would be disappointed by losing.

Some have suggested that no end that implements a nonmoral value can ever sufficiently justify a means that violates a moral rule. This version of the ends–means rule would be the more restricted assertion, "Ends that do not implement moral values cannot justify employing morally wrong means." On these grounds, one might argue that *profit* could never be an end that would justify the means of *deception*. This is certainly a good rule of thumb, but we need to remember that there may be no clear line distinguishing which values are moral and which are nonmoral.

THINK ABOUT IT . . .

"In recent years some very prominent U.S. corporations have been accused of engaging in elaborate deceptions in order to keep their stock prices up. But what's so terrible about deception? In World War II the U.S. and Allies constructed an enormous deception in order to throw the Germans off as to the location of the D-day landings." What are your thoughts on this perspective?

JUSTICE AND FAIRNESS

Not all cases of justification involve showing a relationship between ends and means. Sometimes the process of justifying an action consists in showing that although the action may have appeared wrong, actually it may have been mischaracterized or misunderstood. Here, then, the act of justification is actually a case of clarification. This is frequently what happens when something is characterized as unjust or unfair, and the response—the justification— attempts to show that the activity actually was *fair* or *just*.

Our basic notions of *justice* and *fairness* revolve around the concepts of equal treatment and playing by the rules. It isn't fair to break or bend the rules, and justice isn't done when involved parties are treated unequally.

> *Treating people equally doesn't necessarily mean that everyone receives the* same *treatment.*

Right away, of course, we need to make some distinctions regarding equal treatment. Treating people equally doesn't necessarily mean that everyone receives the *same*. The fact that different employees receive different wages doesn't imply that there is unequal treatment or that an injustice is being done. If Joe and Josh are on the same commission scale and Joe sells twice as much product as Josh, then Joe will get paid more. But this is a case of unequal *results*, not unequal *treatment*. In fact, both men are treated equally inasmuch as the rules are applied to both in exactly the same manner. (Certainly it is possible to believe that justice and fairness require equal results as opposed to equal treatment. It would be beyond the scope of this book to tackle that issue; but, in any event, that seems more of a claim about the rules, rather than their application. See the discussion that follows.)

Clearly, much depends on how we describe the situation and characterize what is being done. From one perspective, people are being treated differently; from another, they are being treated the same. Which is the relevant one? Again, we need to make distinctions. We might say that there is more than one level at which we can ask questions about justice and fairness. At the first level, the relevant question is, "Are we playing by the rules?" or "Are the rules being applied the same way to each person?" Justice requires that no participant is "above the rules," and fairness requires that we play—or act—according to the rules.

At the second level, questions about justice and fairness are questions about *the rules themselves*. At this level, attempting to justify an activity by showing that it is done "according to the rules" will not suffice, because it is the fairness of the rules that is in question.

Imagine the following scenario: Yearly bonuses are awarded on the basis of dollar sales volume, and each sales team generates its volume from within a territory assigned by the regional manager. One team consistently outperforms the others and consistently pockets larger bonuses. The territory assigned to that team has a demonstrably larger base of prospects with significantly greater income potential. Everyone knows this, including the regional manager.

"It's not fair," says a member of a less favored team as the unequal bonuses are distributed, and it is not satisfactory to point out to her that the rules for bonuses have been equally applied to all. What is unfair is not the application of the rules, but the rules themselves—rules that allow the assignment of grossly unequal territories.

We are certainly not attempting here to resolve completely the general question, "How do we determine if rules are fair?" But it would be both relevant and useful to consider a line of thinking suggested by the late John Rawls. Ask yourself the question, "Are these rules that I would choose to live/work/play by?" *But ask that question from the perspective of one who does not know what one's own situation would be for the purpose of the application of the rules.* Would I choose to live by such rules even if I didn't know whether or not I would benefit from them? For example, would a salesperson choose to be governed by the rules in the above example, if that person didn't know whether or not she would be assigned to the favored territory?

Is a set of workplace rules that give preferential treatment to some characteristic (age, sex, race, religion, or whatever) a fair set of rules? Ask yourself if you would choose to be governed by them, *even if you didn't know whether you would possess the relevant characteristic.* It's one thing to be morally comfortable with a set of rules that favor a certain class of persons if you are among that class. But what if you weren't in that class, or didn't know if you would be? Would you choose to live by such a set of rules?

Sometimes our choices or actions appear to be prima facie wrong because of the way they are characterized, and the process of justifying those choices or actions involves showing that they really ought not to be characterized that way. If a system appears to be prima facie wrong because it is unfair, we might justify it by proving that actually it *is* fair. This process often requires that we make careful distinctions and that all parties agree on the way terms are used.

THINK ABOUT IT . . .

Suppose a company had a compensation policy based strictly on longevity (for each position). Would that be fair?

Have you ever been subject to a compensation policy that you thought was unfair? What was unfair about it?

RATIONALIZATIONS AND EXCUSES

So far we have been examining how people may bring forth considerations that will lead us to revise our judgments and to acknowledge that what may appear to be morally wrong really is not so. A related but different line of discussion occurs when an action or choice is acknowledged as prima facie wrong yet "not really so bad." That is, there is not a denial that the action is morally wrong, but it is claimed that something about the circumstances makes this less significant than it would normally be. We have all heard this kind of talk; probably we have all engaged in it at one time or another. It is frequently called *rationalization.*[3]

As with so many of the contrasting terms we use, the key concepts here have no clear dividing line and no exact consistency of usage in real life. For the purposes of our discussion, though, it might be useful to represent things as a continuum.

Justification ————→ Rationalization ————→ Excuse

We have already looked at justification. Rationalization, we might say, occurs when justification fails. Consider a very common response to ethical criticism, namely "everyone does it." Generally, this is not an attempt to justify the action in the sense of showing that it wasn't really wrong. Rather, it is usually put forward as a way of saying that the wrongness, so to speak, is not so serious. The list of rationalizations is as long as the mind is creative: "It didn't hurt anyone"; "There is no law (or written rule) against it"; "No one will ever know"; etc. (This approach borders on the view discussed in Chapter 3, p. 31, that good and bad are determined by what is generally approved or disapproved. If *that* is what is meant, then it is an assertion that the action really wasn't wrong at all.)

---

[3] I am indebted to Michael Josephson, prime mover of the *Character Counts* Coalition, for the idea of including rationalizations in a discussion of ethics, although my treatment of the topic departs from his.

"Oh, sure, it's stolen, but now we have to get on with our lives."

At some point—and here again let us remember that we are not talking about sharp distinctions—rationalizations become excuses. When we offer an excuse for some behavior, we don't really attempt to justify it or minimize its seriousness; rather we seek to point out conditions that would warrant minimizing our punishment or condemnation for it.

"I was desperate; I will never do it again." This statement doesn't suggest that the behavior wasn't really wrong; nor does it discount its seriousness. Instead, it is a way of asking for empathy, mercy, and no punishment. "I had to do it; it was necessary for our company's survival." Again, this is not a denial of wrongdoing; it is a plea for sympathy.

Rationalizations and excuses are not irrelevant in the course of our everyday moral lives. When we are assessing the character of another person, or determining how we are to deal with their misbehavior, it is important to hear them out. Nonetheless we want to remain clear about what we are doing and saying. There certainly may be situations where we decide not to punish someone for what they have done, but that need not imply that we have given approval to the behavior.

Of course we need to listen to ourselves, too. Do the explanations and accounts we give to ourselves really constitute justifications, or do we too frequently rationalize our behavior? Even when we know something is wrong, do we try to convince ourselves that it is really "no big deal," seeking to have our cake and eat it, too?

THINK ABOUT IT . . .

Here are some different responses given to a query about—contrary to policy—using a company car for personal use. Assuming they are all true, how would you classify them in light of the terms just discussed?

- "I had to get my little girl to the emergency room, and it was the only transportation available."

- "Everyone does it."
- "I only used it for an eight-mile round-trip. The cost was negligible."
- "I wouldn't usually do it, but my car broke down and it was my only transportation option to get to the ball game."

Wrap-Up Questions

1. Which of the following statements is/are true?

   A. Ends can always justify means.

   B. Ends can never justify means.

   C. Ends can sometimes justify means.

   D. All of the above.

   E. None of the above.

2. "I know that it was harsh and unfair to take the Switzer account away from Sue. But the client wanted Natasha; and if we hadn't done that, we would have lost the business altogether, and 30 people would have been out of work."

   This is an attempt to

   A. justify.

   B. rationalize.

   C. excuse.

   D. do all of the above.

   E. do none of the above.

3. "Sure we fudged a bit on the fat content, but so does everyone else in the industry."

   This is an example of

   A. justification.

   B. rationalization.

   C. excuse.

   D. all of the above.

   E. none of the above.

4. "Of course our compensation policy is fair. Everyone is treated according to the rules."

   Which assessment seems most correct?

   A. This confuses first- and second-level questions of fairness.

   B. This confuses ends with means.

   C. This confuses rationalizations with excuses.

   D. None of the above.

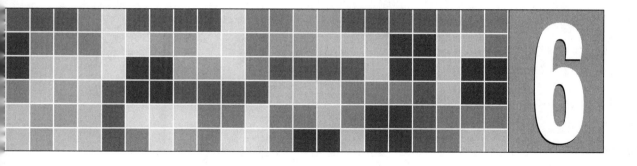

Guidelines for Decision Making

PERFORMANCE GOALS

After completing this chapter, learners will be able to:

■ discuss whether a set of all-purpose procedures can be guaranteed to produce good decisions.

■ list steps to increase the likelihood of making a good decision.

■ indicate that obtaining opinions of others can be helpful, and give examples of why this is true.

■ list three considerations that are important in analyzing the ethical dimensions of a problem or situation.

■ list and discuss ways to define alternatives.

"This might not be ethical. Is that a problem for anybody?"

Warm-Up Questions

1. Which statement do you think is most correct?

   A. In both business and ethics there are strategies and decision-making procedures that can be relied upon always to produce correct decisions.

   B. In business, but not in ethics, there are strategies and decision-making procedures that can be relied upon always to produce correct decisions.

   C. In ethics, but not in business, there are strategies and decision-making procedures that can be relied upon always to produce correct decisions.

   D. In neither business nor ethics are there strategies and decision-making procedures that can be relied upon always to produce correct decisions.

2. Suppose you are in an ethical quandary about a situation at work. Do you think it would be a good idea to seek the counsel of a friend or colleague?

   Yes   No

3. Choose the word or phrase that you think best completes the sentence.

   (A few, Some, Most, All, None) of the ethical issues in business can be settled by referring to professional, organizational, or company codes.

4. "One respect in which ethics and business decisions are alike is that, in both arenas, we want to ignore 'gut' feelings, and stick to analysis and projections."

      Agree   Disagree

5. "It works for business decisions, and it works for ethical decisions. Heck, it works for any kind of decision. You just use the 'Ben Franklin' method. Make two columns. Set out the reasons *for* on one side, and the reasons *against* on the other. Then add them up. The answer will be obvious."

      Agree   Disagree

NO MAGIC FORMULA

It is reasonable to expect that a study of ethics will yield guidelines for making ethical decisions, and it is to such guidelines that our discussion now proceeds. But we want to be careful to avoid two pitfalls. We do not want to oversimplify the subject, nor do we want to overcomplicate it. There are tendencies and temptations in both regards.

We shouldn't expect to be able to construct an ethical decision-making process that allows us to, so to speak, feed the components of our problem into one end and wait for the correct solution to be cranked out at the other. Generally our ethical problems and alternatives are too intertwined and amorphous to be solved in a straightforward computational way.

Not that all ethical issues are complicated. There are "no-brainers" in ethics just as there are in business. Some business choices are pretty easy. Yes, the less expensive, more effective advertising medium is the one you should choose. Moral conclusions aren't *always* hard to come by either. No, it's not morally OK to kill your competitor. (Tempting, maybe, but not OK.)

But, if we think about it, it's as unlikely that we could devise an ethical problem-solving method that would always generate correct answers as it is unlikely that we could construct a business problem-solving method that would always give us the right business decision.

I am reminded of a conversation I had many years ago with a friend in the field of education. He had just been to a conference on the subject of how to teach problem solving. The premise of the sponsors was that education should not focus on facts, figures, and traditional methods. Rather, children should be taught general methods of problem solving so that, armed with such

> *. . . it's as unlikely that we could devise an ethical problem-solving method that would always generate correct answers as it is unlikely that we could construct a business problem-solving method that would always give us the right business decision.*

methods, they would be able to solve problems they would encounter in the future. My friend's query was simply this: If we possess such general problem-solving methods, why should we be content just to teach them to those who will solve the next generation's problems? Why don't we use them now to solve our own?

Of course the answer to his rhetorical question is that we don't use the all-purpose problem-solving method(s), because there is no such method. Neither is there a surefire problem-solving method that we can use in ethics, in business, in personal relationships, or in any other arena.

Still, in ethical matters, as in business and other activities of life, to say that we can't provide a 100 percent guaranteed method for making decisions does not mean that we have nothing to go on at all. We have a variety of strategies, checklists, and other methods that help us often, though not always, come up with good solutions to complicated situations.

Sports enthusiasts are familiar with all sorts of rules of thumb ("pass on third down and long yardage," "with three balls and no strikes, take the next pitch," "move up on second serve") that, if followed, will generally yield successful results. They don't *always* work, but they are still very useful. They employ the percentages.

Similarly, retailers employ pricing strategies, salespeople have closing techniques, investment advisers use time-tested formulas, and so on. In every business and every activity, we can find guidelines and strategies for success. The shelves of bookstores are stuffed to overflowing with them. While some are certainly better than others, none is perfect. Nor, really, do we expect any to be. Neither should we expect an ethics decision-making guide that is guaranteed to be 100 percent successful.

> *. . . we cannot overemphasize how useful and important it can be to obtain the counsel and opinions of others.*

With that caveat we turn to some suggested steps—a checklist, if you will—to be used in a situation when it isn't clear what is the ethically correct thing to do. In all of these it cannot be overemphasized how useful and important it can be to obtain the counsel and opinions of others. It's just a fact: our friends and our colleagues are often capable of seeing and sensing things we might miss. And frequently they can add a perspective we may lack.

THINK ABOUT IT . . .

"Always do the right thing. This will gratify some and astonish the rest."
—Mark Twain
Do you think it is true that we always know what is the right thing to do?

IDENTIFY THE ISSUES

Unfortunately, many of the ethical problems we confront are not labeled as such. It is easy to be so focused on the financial, marketing, production, technical, or other issues before us that we never even see the ethical dimension to the alternatives we are considering. This is one of the reasons that it is a good idea to draw on the counsel of others. They may notice things that have escaped our attention.

Recall the point that many ethical issues related to the medical field—concerns that seem commonplace today—originated in practices that, innocently enough, were never considered morally questionable. These issues range from informed consent and the rights of patients to matters of resource allocation (e.g., "Do some *deserve* a donated organ more than others?"; "How much of limited funds should be spent to treat those whose chosen living habits have left them chronically ill?").

In similar fashion we can look at corporate and business practices that today are brightly lit on the moral radar screen, whereas once they were never even a subject of question. Pollution, discrimination, insider trading, and price-fixing all represent practices to which, at one time, no one gave much thought, if any. Yet now there is widespread agreement that such behavior is unethical as well as illegal.[1] An interesting question to ask ourselves today is, "What do we do now that is generally thought acceptable that in 20 or 30 years (perhaps less) may be seen as ethically objectionable and something that ought to be prohibited?"

> *. . . we can look at corporate and business practices that today are brightly lit on the moral radar screen, whereas once they were never even a subject of question.*

For these reasons, although it may sound too obvious, one of the most important aspects of ethical decision making is, at the outset, to determine if there are ethical issues involved in the course of action being considered. There are three useful practices in this regard.

1. Refer to Rules, Codes, and the Law

Again, this suggestion may seem obvious, but unfortunately it is easily overlooked. It is sometimes too easy or tempting to dismiss various rules and codes, even the law, as outdated or unimportant in a particular

---

[1] We want to be careful here not to say that such practices are wrong because they are (now) illegal. Rather, they have become illegal because they were *first* perceived to be wrong. A system of rules that allows such things is/was thought to be unfair and unjust because it results in harm to innocent parties. For that reason we adopt rules to prevent the behavior in question. The creation of laws is not arbitrary, and it often is the result of a moral perception.

> *. . . it is important to remember that rules and codes come to be for a reason, and if they are broken or ignored, a justification will be necessary.*

circumstance. While I would be the last to argue that the whole of morality lies in "following the rules," it is important to remember that rules and codes come to be for a reason, and if they are broken or ignored, a justification will be necessary.

Corporate and professional codes can be valuable in this regard. For one thing, they may keep us from having to reinvent the wheel when faced with a particular situation. For example, IBM employees don't have to engage in an ethical calculation to determine whether it is all right to accept a gift from a supplier. The company code tells them straightforwardly not to. (I am not claiming here that it would always be wrong for anyone in any company to accept a gift from a supplier. The point is rather that a "zero tolerance no-gifts rule," while possibly ruling out certain innocuous exchanges, leans to the side of caution so that, if it is followed, an employee will not get caught in a situation that has negative features.) Even if company and professional codes are somewhat vague, as they often are, they can still be useful by pointing employees in the right direction and encouraging them to ask the proper questions.

Conversely, we should remember that just because a particular course of action does not clearly violate some rule, it is not therefore ethically acceptable or desirable. "Legal has cleared it" doesn't necessarily mean it's a right thing to do.

Often the law and other sets of rules provide only a minimum standard. Good ethics may require more. In the famous case of the Johnson & Johnson recall of Tylenol, the company was not compelled by the law to act as it did. Rather, Johnson & Johnson pulled the product because the company thought it was the right thing to do.[2]

2. Identify Stakeholders and Their Interests

The term *stakeholders* has come to refer to all those involved with and affected by a decision or course of action. They are those who, as we say, have a stake in the decision. It is a play on *stockholders* to be sure, and that play helps to make the point that a corporation will likely have to consider more interests than just those of the stockholders if it is to act in an ethically responsible manner.

---

[2] For an account of the Tylenol event see, for example, "Johnson & Johnson and the Tylenol Case" in De George, *Business Ethics*, 3–4. Interestingly, this was a situation where Johnson & Johnson's laudable behavior was a result of its long-held code, The Credo, which in its leaders' eyes required action beyond that demanded by law.

DILBERT reprinted by permission of United Feature Syndicate, Inc.

While the lists of stakeholders vary in different situations, often they include such diverse groups as employees and their families, suppliers, customers, and certain affected communities. The net may be cast so wide as to include *the environment* as a stakeholder in the decisions that some companies might make.

An analysis of stakeholder interests calls for an imaginative and empathetic understanding of the various groups and the ways in which they may be impacted. In this respect, the thinking required to arrive at a good ethical decision is closely related to the kind of thinking involved in making a good business decision. Good businesses understand their customers, their vendors, and their employees. Ignoring the interests of any of these can be bad business as well as bad ethics.

> *An analysis of stakeholder interests calls for an imaginative and empathetic understanding of the various groups and the ways in which they may be impacted.*

3. Apply the "Gut Check"

We've all had the feeling at one time or another that something just isn't right. We find ourselves uneasy about something we're about to do, yet we can't articulate exactly what the problem is.

I'm not referring to a distinctly or exclusively moral sixth sense here. This kind of qualm occurs in nonmoral situations as well. You're about to make a big purchase or invest a significant amount of money. You think you've done all your homework, and every indicator says "go"; yet still you are uneasy.

We might call this a test of our feelings, and it has many versions. In the ethical context some would ask, "Having done this, would you be comfortable looking at yourself in the mirror?" Others suggest you should ask

> *"Having done this, would you be comfortable looking at yourself in the mirror?"*

"*Miss Dugan, will you send someone in here who can distinguish right from wrong?*"

yourself if you would want your mother, or your kids, to know what you are thinking of doing. Or would you want your action to be reported in the newspaper? Some would say that a negative answer to such questions, and that feeling of unease about a proposed course of action, are our *conscience* speaking. Be that as it may, we do well to pay heed.

Feelings such as this do not determine that a decision is wrong (either practically or morally) any more than finding that something is within the rules makes it right. But such feelings deserve our attention. Indeed, as we strive to cultivate moral character, we may discover that such feelings and reactions turn out to be on target, even if we have not articulated the reasons for them.

SITUATION ANALYSIS

We have noted earlier that in ethics, as in business, our greatest impediment to good decision making is often *lack of information*. Sometimes the information that we need is analytical in nature, information that may help to clarify the situation or categorize the alternatives being considered. At other times the information needed may be empirical or factual. We may require technical information, market research, or cost analysis, for instance.

1. Develop Information

In sorting out the ethical dimensions of an issue, we need to develop information that will enable us to evaluate alternatives. If one method of achieving an objective involves violating some moral, institutional, or statutory rule, is there another way of reaching the goal without rule breaking? Are we faced with a situation where our duties conflict? Do we have conflicting obligations to different constituencies? Can we determine what values should guide us in resolving the conflicts?

Our analysis of stakeholder interests will require factual information in order to determine what consequences various alternatives would have for different groups. This is why it is so important to know our stakeholders. We need to know more than who they are; we need to know—as best we can—how they would likely be affected by one alternative or another.

> ... it is so important to know our stakeholders.

Suppose we are considering adopting mandatory drug testing for the employees of our company.[3] There are analytical questions to ask. Would such a policy be within the law? Would it violate the rights of any employee? Would it conflict with any union agreements or employment contracts? Would such a policy conflict with any stated company values regarding mutual trust and respect? There are also factual, empirical questions to ask, although we may only be able to give "best guess" answers. Even if such a policy is legal and not in violation of any previous commitments, would it breed employee resentment that might outweigh the business benefits of the policy? Would adopting this policy result in a positive or negative reaction from such stakeholders as our customers and our stockholders? Might the results of drug testing lead to more harm for (certain) employees than good for the company?

THINK ABOUT IT . . .

Can you think of a situation in which you were a stakeholder in a decision, but the interests of you and those in your situation were not taken into account? Did you think there was anything wrong with that? How should it have been handled?

---

[3] For a much more thoroughly elaborated example of the issues that could arise in such a situation, see "Drug Testing at College International" in Tom L. Beauchamp, *Case Studies in Business, Society, and Ethics*, 4th ed. (Upper Saddle River, NJ: Prentice Hall, 1998), 260–64, and also "Case 1: Drug and Polygraph Testing at Company X" in De George, *Business Ethics*, 387–88.

2. Define Alternatives

> . . . as we ask questions about the value implications and the potential consequences of a proposed course of action, we may even come to a better understanding of the original problem . . .

Asking questions such as these helps us define our alternatives, and sometimes reshape our proposals. Indeed, as we ask questions about the value implications and the potential consequences of a proposed course of action, we may even come to a better understanding of the original problem and the goals of the solution.

The proposal imagined above, to adopt mandatory drug testing for employees, might have originated in any of a variety of different perceptions. It might have stemmed from a belief that drug use within the employee population was affecting production *quality*. Or perhaps some believed that drug use was causing supervisory and managerial *inefficiency*. The suggestion could have arisen from a genuine concern about employee welfare. Alternatively, the policy proposal might have been motivated simply by a desire to reap public relations benefits in a community where "zero tolerance" sentiments were both strong and widespread. The proposal might have come from a mix of these beliefs, and, of course, there might have been other considerations as well. Becoming clearer about the problem(s) we are trying to solve helps us define our alternative solutions.

ANALYZE AND COMPARE THE ALTERNATIVES

> . . . we intuitively know that some reasons outweigh other ones, but we usually have no protocol for assigning weights to them.

Most of us have heard of the decision-making process (and sales-closing technique) that involves writing down the reasons *for* doing something on one side of a vertical line and the reasons *against* doing it on the other. This can be a useful exercise, although anyone who has actually tried it knows that it doesn't yield a straightforward decision. That is because we intuitively know that some reasons outweigh other ones, but we usually have no protocol for assigning weights to them. Hence, even if we have written down all the reasons, we can't simply add them up.

From an ethical perspective, comparing alternative courses of action is similar. While it is good and important to compare alternatives, we usually can't assign exact values to the issues that might lead us to favor one action over another.

1. Compare the Consequences

As much as possible we must compare the various *consequences* of the possibilities we are considering. Tom Morris makes the following trenchant comment about his realization upon reviewing times in his life when he did things he later came to regard as ethically wrong: "[I]n every case I had failed to imagine vividly and perceptively the full consequences of my actions for other people as well as for myself. I had put blinders on my moral imagination and had seen in advance only those consequences that I wanted to see."[4]

Of course we can't know *for sure* what the consequences of our choices will be, and that is true in virtually any situation. We just do the best we can, in ethics, in business, and in life.

2. Consider the Values at Issue

Consequences, of course, have to be considered from a certain perspective. Namely, we need to consider the consequences of various alternatives in light of the *values* that we seek to implement. And we may need to rank those values.

If we were pretty sure that adopting (some version of) a drug-testing policy would result in a high level of employee dissatisfaction, then, assuming that good employee morale is a value of our organization, that would be a reason not to do it. But the consequences of *not* adopting the policy might serve to undermine some other value, such as product quality or even employee safety. And those values might be more important than employee morale.

Of course, this example is not meant to imply that such an issue would actually have to come down to an *either/or* proposition. One can imagine a number of nuanced alternatives that might serve to foster all the values we seek to implement.

3. Apply the "Gut Test" Again

We want to re-apply a test that is relevant when a choice or situation is first proposed to us. Whether we call it the "look in the mirror" test, the "would you want your mother to know you did this" test, or the "how would you like this to be in the newspapers" test, it all comes down to asking ourselves how we *feel* about doing the action under consideration.

Again, this is not to appeal to some mystical faculty with which we are endowed. The reactions that we have are a result of the training we have received and the culture(s) in which we have developed. If we seem to

> *The reactions that we have are a result of the training we have received and the culture(s) in which we have developed.*

---

[4] Morris, *If Aristotle Ran General Motors* (New York: Henry Holt and Co. Owl Books, 1998), 166.

be appealing to moral intuition, let us acknowledge that such intuition is *informed*. More particularly, it is formed in us as a result of experiences as diverse as the lessons we received in childhood, the experiences we have had in "the real world" of business, and the discussions that might occur in a corporate training session.

4. Try the Golden Rule Test

Finally, there is the Golden Rule test: Is this the sort of thing I would want done to me? Would I want to be treated in such a fashion? But here we have to be careful how we frame the issue. We can illustrate this point by considering an example without moral overtones.

The principle of the Golden Rule rests at the heart of good manners and what is generally thought of as considerate treatment of others. If you have people over for dinner you don't just serve what you like, you give some consideration to what they like. You may like liver and onions, but you probably won't find many others who do. Now if you served liver and onions to a group of dinner guests, could you say you were following the Golden Rule because you treated them as you would have them treat you? Hardly. The problem is that we have framed the issue incorrectly by focusing on the outcome, rather than the principle. The principle would be "serve people what they like." That is a principle by which you would want to be treated, even if in this case it results in a different outcome for others.

> *. . . the Golden Rule test should be applied to the* principle *we adopt, not to the* outcomes *it yields.*

If, to return to a more serious sphere, we were forced to devise a principle for layoffs, the Golden Rule test should be applied to the *principle* we adopt, not to the *outcomes* it yields. Presumably none of us wants to be laid off, and if we focused on outcome we would always say, "No, I wouldn't want that done to me." But if we focus on the principle, and the principle is a fair one, we could answer, "Yes, that is a way I would want to be treated," even if the treatment might result in a personally undesirable outcome.

CONCLUSION

By way of conclusion I would reiterate two points. One, there is no one simple (or even complex) formula for arriving at ethical decisions. Not all ethical problems are the same, and many of them are complex. They require us to consider ethical dimensions to situations while we are also thinking of nitty-gritty issues such as profitability, production schedules, performance reviews, and the like. But while we can't simply compute ethical answers, we can approach matters by asking questions and applying perspectives such as the ones discussed here.

The second point is that we cannot overemphasize the value of sharing our thoughts with others and seeking the counsel of those we know and respect. While our decisions must be our own, remember that our values are played out, so to speak, in a community. The perspectives of others can frequently provide us with greater insight into that community.

THINK ABOUT IT . . .

Suppose your company has found it necessary to lay off one-fifth of its personnel in each division. There are no constraints as to the manner in which this is to occur. Devise a policy that in your mind will satisfy both ethical concerns and the company's economic requirements.

Wrap-Up Questions

1. Which statement is most correct?

   A. In both business and ethics, there are strategies and decision-making procedures that can be relied upon always to produce correct decisions.

   B. In business, but not in ethics, there are strategies and decision-making procedures that can be relied upon always to produce correct decisions.

   C. In ethics, but not in business, there are strategies and decision-making procedures that can be relied upon always to produce correct decisions.

   D. In both business and ethics, there are strategies and decision-making procedures that can be relied upon to increase the likelihood of making correct decisions.

2. In ethics, as in business, there are no easy decisions.

   True   False

3. When faced with complex or difficult ethical decisions,

   A. you should always consult with the stakeholders.

   B. don't let yourself be influenced by your friends.

   C. try to overcome your instinctive reactions.

   D. do all of the above.

   E. do none of the above.

4. The BDL Company archives all email that goes out of and into company computers, and it maintains a record of all Internet use. At any time, the information technology department can access the screen of any user. It was a deliberate management decision that the employees of BDL not be made aware of these company practices and capabilities.

Which statement seems most correct?

A. This is another example of the means being used to justify the ends.

B. Employees were stakeholders in this decision.

C. A decision such as this one is best made without consultation.

D. All of the above.

E. None of the above.

5. When a businessperson is confronted with a decision that has ethical implications, the Golden Rule test applies to

A. customers.

B. executives.

C. employees.

D. stockholders.

E. all of the above.

F. none of the above.

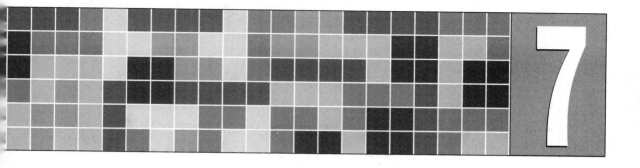

Individual Traits and Character

PERFORMANCE GOALS

After completing this chapter, learners will be able to:

- discuss how our training influences our responses to situations.
- define character.
- indicate how habit and choice are related.
- define virtues and give examples.
- define integrity and describe a person who has integrity.
- state what it means to have honor.
- discuss why having a regard for others is essential to ethical living.

"Don't you dare ever mention the word INTEGRITY in this office again!"

Warm-Up Questions

1. "Doing the right thing" generally requires rising above one's day-to-day character.

     Agree   Disagree

2. Which word or phrase do you think best completes the sentence?

(Anyone, No one, Only a few, Most people) can change their habits of behavior.

3. "*Virtue* is an outmoded concept, suitable only to a bygone era."

     Agree   Disagree

4. If there's one essential trait needed to live an ethical life, it would be

    A. caring for others as much as yourself.

    B. caring for others more than yourself.

    C. always taking others into consideration.

    D. looking out for yourself first, and then taking others into consideration.

    E. all of the above.

    F. none of the above.

5. Categorize each character trait as:
   A. desirable in all contexts;
   B. desirable only in some contexts;
   C. undesirable only in some contexts; or
   D. undesirable in all contexts.

_____ innovative	_____ friendly	_____ sensitive	_____ jealous
_____ careful	_____ trustworthy	_____ objective	_____ efficient
_____ selfish	_____ loyal	_____ fair	_____ empathetic
_____ uncaring	_____ generous	_____ hotheaded	_____ sentimental
_____ cautious	_____ humble	_____ outgoing	_____ focused
_____ cruel	_____ competitive	_____ considerate	_____ dishonest
_____ aggressive	_____ self-centered		

In discussing such things as ethical principles, judgments, justification, and decision making, our focus has been on the intellectual or analytical aspects of ethics. But by that I do not mean to draw a contrast with *feelings*. Rather I mean to draw the contrast with what might be called the *behavioral* aspect of ethics—the way someone lives and acts that results both in and from the kind of person he or she is.

Ethics is a matter of how we live, not simply what we know. Our discussion of ethics would be seriously incomplete if it only treated the topics covered thus far. (It would also fail were it to result only in "head knowledge.") To complete our task we need to talk about behavior and character.

> *Ethics is a matter of how we live, not simply what we know.*

THE DEVELOPMENT OF CHARACTER

A Marine fighter pilot once told me, "People don't 'rise to the occasion'; they default to the level of their training." He was talking about aerial combat, but his statement applies to ethical behavior as well. (It applies to sports and sales, too. Indeed, what does it *not* apply to?)

To be sure, all of us will now scratch our heads thinking up some exception to this "rule," but the point in general remains a valid one. Our responses to events and situations, be they "gut reactions" or reflectively considered, do not come out of nowhere. They arise from our character, our professional persona, our role as a parent, husband, wife, and so on. And *who we are* in those respects is a result of what we have been taught and what we have been trained and have trained ourselves to be.

Trained ourselves to be? Now that is an odd expression to say the least. But it is vitally important. It points to the paradoxical but central fact of character development: that, although what we do is a result of who and what we are, we also *become what we do.*

Many of us have been exposed to this principle in one kind of professional setting or other. It is the grist of the trainer's mill. Do you want to be an organized person? Act like organized people do. Do organized things. Categorize tasks, write things down in a systematic way (not on sticky notes all over your desk, wall, and computer), schedule tasks, and so forth.

Is confidence a trait that you seek? Act the way confident people do! Shake hands firmly, maybe even using the type A, over-the-top method. Practice looking people in the eye. Visualize your successful outcomes. Speak of your achievements, both those accomplished and those to come. Follow this advice—and the rest of the tips found in the books and tapes—and you will find that you have made yourself a confident person!

> *"People don't 'rise to the occasion'; they default to the level of their training."*

I don't mean to sound too satirical; for the truth is—as many of us no doubt know—there is validity in these approaches. People who take the advice and put the habit-building behaviors into action do actually change themselves, sometimes in significant ways. The rub, of course, is that you really have to take the advice and *do* something, not just hear it.

Our character, in both the moral dimension and otherwise, is a summary of our habits of behavior. When you attribute a character trait—cheerfulness, kindness, trustworthiness—to someone, you are saying that this is the way in which that person habitually acts. You can expect that kind of behavior from him or her.

There is both bad news and good news in this. The bad news is that, as we must all know, habits (mostly bad ones, it seems) are easily, often unconsciously formed and can be difficult to break. The good news is that we *can* break old habits and we *can* instill new ones, and we *can* cause ourselves to become the sort of person we aspire to be.

> *. . . we are constantly training ourselves to be certain types of people.*

Anyone who has experienced parenthood knows that parents are constantly training their children to be certain kinds of persons, whether the training is intentional or not. Curiously, the same is true of each of us individually. That is, we are constantly training ourselves to be certain types of people. Mostly this is done unconsciously. We just keep doing the same kinds of things we have been doing, and we reinforce the habitual behavior instilled in us long ago. Occasionally, though, we will consciously seek to effect change, whether by breaking an old habit or adopting a new one; and when we do that we literally change our character.

Once again, Tom Morris speaks eloquently:

Too many people in high places talk big about ethics, and morality, and virtue, and goodness, but do not practice these qualities when they interact day-to-day with the people who work for them. There are far too many people who want to increase the general weal of the world without doing the unglamorous and sometimes inconvenient work of, for example, responding in kindness to a coworker during a time of stress. The little kindnesses, the small decencies, form the foundation for truly magnificent things.[1]

UCLA basketball coach John Wooden was famous for his emphasis on the fundamentals. His players achieved great victories and turned in outstanding performances because they had been trained to do the little things, the basic things, habitually in the right way. An application of the same principle to moral character development can produce similar results. If we train ourselves to do the little things correctly—for instance, to take others into account, to speak the truth, to play by the rules (even if no one is watching)—we prepare ourselves and develop the kind of character that will take the big things in stride. Without cultivating such habits, without training ourselves, we are not likely to rise to the occasion.

THINK ABOUT IT . . .

Give an example, involving either you or someone you know, of a person changing, adopting, or breaking a habit of behavior. What did it take to make this happen?

CHARACTER TRAITS AND VIRTUES

William Bennett notwithstanding, we don't talk about *virtues* much anymore.[2] The term has a quaint Victorian sound to it. When it is used, it more likely than not occurs in a nonmoral context, as in, "The virtue of his presentations is that they are clear and brief." But we need not be put off by, or wary of, talk about virtues in the moral sense. The term does not invoke some inscrutable ethical aura, nor does it commit us to the adoption of some particular code, perhaps now outmoded.

Virtues, as we use the term here, simply refers to character traits (good ones, that is; *vices* is reserved for the other end of the spectrum). And, as we have noted, such traits need not always be thought of as uniquely associated with ethics or morality. *Friendliness* holds a place among the classic virtues, and though it may not fit into our conception of what constitutes good moral character, few would argue against its desirability as a character trait.

---

[1] *If Aristotle Ran General Motors*, 164.

[2] Well, most of us don't. Actually there are a number of philosophers—people like Tom Morris and Robert Solomon—who speak of virtue, and do so quite well. Morris's and Solomon's focus on the role of virtue in business might do little to reintroduce virtue terminology into the popular vocabulary, but they have probably had considerable influence in making some business environments better places to be.

Many virtues are role related. Aggressiveness might be a desirable trait in a professional athlete, but not such a wonderful thing for a family counselor. Other traits, such as trustworthiness, seem to cut across all categories. Moreover, not only does a trait such as trustworthiness have a moral dimension to it, it also has business value. (We've all had experiences with an untrustworthy businessperson. Whom do you prefer to deal with?)

Our aim here is certainly not to try to create a list of all the behavioral habits that might be considered virtues. Nor is it to catalog various traits as to which ones have a distinct moral value, which are desirable only for situation-specific reasons, which seem desirable in any setting, and so on. Rather we want simply to emphasize that the components of good character are habits of behavior. As such, they lie within the grasp of any of us; for it is within our power to form our habits. The Nike slogan applies to ethics, too: "Just do it."

> . . . the components of good character are habits of behavior. As such, they lie within the grasp of any of us . . .

1. Integrity and Honor

We use words like "honor," "code," and "loyalty." We use these words as the backbone of a life spent defending something. You use them as a punch line.

—Jack Nicholson, as Col. Nathan Jessup, in *A Few Good Men*

Although a dictionary won't show that *integrity* and *honor* are synonyms, they are often treated as if they denote the same qualities. To say that someone is a person of "honor and integrity" seems to say the same thing twice. Certainly the terms are closely related, and it is appropriate to discuss them together.

Integrity

Integrity does not seem a virtue in itself; rather, having this characteristic is more the *result* of virtues—of having acquired them. If someone displays the character traits of honesty, trustworthiness, fairness, and so on—if he or she habitually behaves in these ways—then, as a result, we will say that this is a person of integrity. The person can be counted on to behave in those ways. He or she is not likely to be buffeted by the winds of circumstance or swayed by a conflicting self-interest.

> A person of integrity is not likely to be buffeted by the winds of circumstance or swayed by a conflicting self-interest.

The word *integrity* derives from a root that means *whole* (think of *integer*), and it has uses in nonmoral as well as moral contexts. Indeed, there is something to be learned by looking at the nonmoral uses. When we speak of the integrity of a building or a material, we mean that the thing in question is strong or solid, that it can be counted on to do what it is supposed to do. Certainly the ascription of moral integrity to someone carries a similar meaning.

The wholeness of integrity comes about from the unification of principles and action. A consistency of belief and behavior characterizes a person of integrity. This is why one dictionary says that *hypocrisy* is a "failure of integrity."

None of this, though, should imply that people of integrity are some otherworldly saintly creatures, or that they have all the answers when it comes to questions of ethics and morality. To the contrary, people of integrity are liable to perceive and feel the weight of moral dilemmas more than most. Not all ethical dilemmas, after all, are simply matters of weighing principle against self-interest. (Frankly, in most cases *that* is not a dilemma at all. An issue of temptation and a test of character perhaps, but not a dilemma.) The nature of many moral dilemmas consists in a conflict of rules. Sometimes, as we have noted, general moral principles may conflict. Moreover, because our jobs and positions often carry with them particular obligations (e.g., company loyalty, fiduciary duty, nondisclosure, etc.), moral quandaries may occur when our positional duties and obligations conflict with more general ones. People of integrity can be counted on to fulfill their duties and follow the rules that apply to them; but even they—especially they—may find that they need to sort out which rules and which duties are the overriding ones.

> *. . . people of integrity are liable to perceive and feel the weight of moral dilemmas more than most.*

Honor

Boy Scouts and Girl Scouts say a pledge that begins, "On my honor . . . " The signers of the Declaration of Independence pledged "our lives, our fortunes, and our sacred honor." When I was in college each exam, paper, or project we submitted contained a cover pledge, "On my honor as a gentleman . . . ," that we had neither

> *Whether we live with honor or not is up to us. No one can give us honor but ourselves; and no one else can take it away.*

At their initial meeting, a lawyer tells his prospective client that he will need a $1,000 retainer if he is going to take on the situation. That is fine with the client, and at their next meeting he hands the lawyer an envelope. "Here is the retainer. It's in cash. I hope that is OK." The lawyer says "yes," and they proceed onto business.

When the client leaves the lawyer opens the envelope and counts the money. The envelope contains eleven $100 bills. Now the lawyer has a moral dilemma: Should he tell his partner? [Relax: It's a joke.]

given nor received assistance—that the work was our own. What is the common thread that runs through these uses of *honor*? What does the term refer to?

The dictionary tells us that honor is *esteem* or *respect* that is *due or paid to worth*. To honor someone is to hold them in esteem or respect. When we honor a person we ascribe worth of some sort to them. We may honor or give honors to someone for athletic prowess, achievements, bravery, or any manner of other doings. But how does this relate to one's personal honor, the honor on which one pledges?

> *. . . the person who has honor ascribes worth to him- or herself.*

As the act of honoring another is to ascribe worth to them, the person who *has* honor ascribes worth to him- or herself. (Conversely, I believe, the person who lacks a sense of honor is a person who lacks a sense of self-worth.) This worth is based on character, not skills. Thus honor is not equivalent to integrity, but it derives from it. A person who has honor, or a sense of honor, is a person who lives by a code or a set of principles, and who finds such value in so doing that he or she counts it as a basis of self-worth.

Just as the principles involved in a given individual's integrity may be ones that derive from his or her role or position, similarly one's sense of honor may be intimately tied to one's station. It is common—to the extent that language about honor is common—that the term is followed by a characterizing expression: "On my honor as . . . " a knight, a gentleman, a doctor, an officer, etc. Thus stated, one puts one's integrity on the line as a follower of a certain code or set of principles.

One of Tom Clancy's characters relays the thought that honor is "a man's gift to himself." Although this gender-insensitive formulation may not be politically correct, the notion is a sound one. Whether we live with honor or not is up to us. No one can give us honor but ourselves, and no one else can take it away.

THINK ABOUT IT . . .

"Honor is an outmoded concept that depends on antiquated moral codes. It is irrelevant to life in the twenty-first century."

What do *you* think of this view?

2. Regard for Others

If there is one character trait that might be deemed essential for ethical living, it would have to be the habit of considering others' thoughts, feelings, and welfare when contemplating a decision or course of action. No single word appears to quite capture this idea. It is, for want of a better expression, the quality of being *other-regarding*.

This is a characteristic that goes beyond being considerate. *Considerate* seems to apply only to fairly close, personal interactions. The characteristic of being other-regarding may cast the net much farther than that. It takes into account, when appropriate, whole classes of people, perhaps people not even personally known to the agent. It denotes the habit of paying heed to the potential effect of actions on employees, customers, suppliers, and vendors—in short, all stakeholders. A person need not be in the business arena for this kind of thinking to be relevant. Anyone who lives and acts in a community—a coach, a family member, a neighbor—will be a better person to the extent that his or her behavior encompasses a regard for others.

A person who is other-regarding is not by virtue of that necessarily insensitive to rules, duties, and obligations. Not at all. But such a person will always want to know more than simply, "Is this what the rules say?" or "Is this something the rules allow?" "Who will be affected, and how?" will always be a relevant consideration, too.

Nor should we think that to be other-regarding is necessarily to sublimate one's own self-interest to the interests of others. The characteristic of taking others into account goes to the bedrock of ethical conduct, namely the notion that *everyone counts*. But to say that is to say that you, I, we count too.

Ethics does not require self-denial, and ethical behavior is not measured by the degree to which one becomes a doormat. There is nothing inherently unethical about living and conducting business in a way that enhances one's own self-interest. But neither does the advancement of self-interest allow one to break rules, ignore duties, or disregard the well-being of others.

> *Ethics does not require self-denial; and ethical behavior is not measured by the degree to which one becomes a doormat.*

The characteristic of being other-regarding is the behavioral embodiment of the Golden Rule. It is the habit of "putting ourselves into the other person's shoes." It is asking, "Would I want this done to me?" It acknowledges our basic equality and is central to ethical living.

THINK ABOUT IT . . .

"The idea of living ethically is basically contrary to human nature, for ethics requires that we must deny our own self-interest, and no one does that." What do *you* think of such a statement?

Wrap-Up Questions

1. Marcia is the type of boss who is not only demanding but also abusive. She is known for her yelling tirades, and there are countless stories of her publicly demeaning subordinates who she believed were not performing up to her standards.

   Which of the following statements is most correct?

   A. From this, we know enough to make inferences about the productivity of Marcia's department.
   B. We can infer that it is not likely that Marcia takes all stakeholders into account when making a policy decision.
   C. It is likely that Marcia is dishonest.
   D. All of the above.
   E. None of the above.

2. If she chose to, Marcia could probably learn not to be so abusive to subordinates.

   True   False

3. Which of the following statements is correct?

   A. Certain character traits may be considered virtues in some contexts, but not in all.
   B. Not all virtues are ethical virtues.
   C. Some ethical virtues are also valuable character traits in business.
   D. All of the above.
   E. None of the above.

4. If a company has a reputation for integrity,

   A. it can be expected to stand behind its products and/or services.
   B. its products and/or services will always be the best priced in the marketplace.
   C. its products and/or services will always outperform the competition.
   D. all of the above.
   E. none of the above.

5. Living ethically requires that you always put the interests of others before your own.

   True   False

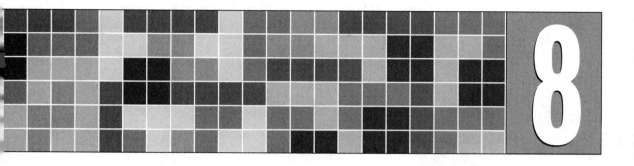

Corporate Character and the Role of Leadership

PERFORMANCE GOALS

After completing this chapter, learners will be able to:

- describe character development and how it can be enhanced.
- describe the role of leadership in supporting development of good character.
- name various leadership roles and the characteristics they need.
- indicate the tasks of leadership with regard to an organization's values.
- discuss values training and methods for providing it.

*"It's an amazing coincidence, isn't it, that we all
served on the same board of directors?"*

Warm-Up Questions

1. An organization can have the effect of making people who belong to it
better.

    Agree   Disagree

2. Which statement seems the most correct to you?

  A. Just as an organization may have many levels of management, it
     may have many levels of leadership.

  B. Large organizations may have many managers, but they can have
     only one leader.

  C. Businesses don't have leaders; they have bosses and/or managers.

  D. All of the above.

  E. None of the above.

3. The job of communicating a company's values to its employees
   A. is best accomplished by professional experts.
   B. can't be done by management.
   C. has to start at the top.
   D. starts from the bottom up.
   E. is best done implicitly, rather than explicitly.
   F. All of the above.
   G. None of the above.

4. "A company that is really serious about ethics and values would require the *same* training for *all* of its employees, including management."

       Agree   Disagree

5. "Leadership can't be accomplished by example, because those who are leaders will have very different jobs from those who are to be led."

       Agree   Disagree

THE INFLUENCE OF INSTITUTIONS

Most of what I know about honor I learned from two distinctly different institutions: Princeton University and the United States Marine Corps. (The manner in which these institutions are *similar* is worthy of a commentary in its own right.) The point of this observation is not to convey biographical information; rather it is to emphasize the role of institutions in the inculcation of values and the development of character.

To be more precise, I should say that I learned about honor *at* these institutions more than *from* them. There were no lectures on honor, no explicit lessons, no designated classes. And yet, what was expected of us, what behaviors we were to conform to, what standards we were to uphold were an ever-present part of the cultural milieu.

The previous chapter emphasized the capacities of individuals to shape and form their own characters. Yet it would be both misleading and disingenuous not also to acknowledge that character development, even more character *change*, is unlikely unless it occurs in an environment with cultural and institutional support. It would be pretty hard to diet if you spent most of your time hanging out with members of the gourmet club. Conversely, as many well-known diet programs have proven, it is easier to change your eating behavior when you have the support and encouragement of others who share the same goals.

"You play better golf with better golfers." The adage applies to much more than golf, and to much more than sports. Do you want to improve your sales performance?

> *"You play better golf with better golfers." The adage applies to much more than golf, and to much more than sports.*

DILBERT reprinted by permission of United Feature Syndicate, Inc.

Associate with top producers. Do you want to develop a more positive attitude? Surround yourself with positive people. Robert Solomon offers a modern version of the ancient Greek saying "To live the good life one must live in a great city," when he advises his business students who seek to live morally decent professional lives to "choose the right company."[1] And there is an institutional corollary to that advice: "If you want to have a company characterized by integrity and high ethical standards, hire good people."

Recall the paradoxical but central fact regarding character: our behavior arises out of our character, while at the same time our character is formed by our behavior. The same rule applies to the relationship between individuals and the organizations to which they belong. Ultimately the character of an organization is determined by the people who are a part of it; yet it is the institution that enhances and enables the development of the persons associated with it.

Fans knew of the fantastic won/lost record of John Wooden's UCLA teams, but basketball players knew more. They knew that they would become better players if they became a part of his program. The "wizard of Westwood" recruited great athletes, to be sure, but they improved as they benefited from participating in an organization under his leadership. Players who had been all-American quality in high school were willing to sit on the bench during their first college years because they knew they stood a better chance of becoming pros under Wooden's program than if they had started as a star somewhere else.

Playing with good players will increase your own performance level. Working with sharp, productive people will improve your own professional skills. And operating in an environment where integrity is valued and prin-

---

[1] Solomon, "Corporate Roles, Personal Virtues," in *Ethical Issues in Business: A Philosophical Approach*, 7th ed., ed. Thomas Donaldson, Patricia H. Werhane, Margaret Cording (Upper Saddle River, N.J.: Prentice Hall, 2002), 75.

ciples are upheld will develop and enhance your own sense of honor and morality.

THINK ABOUT IT . . .

Have you ever been associated with an institution that in some way made you a better person than you would have been if you had not been a part of it? Or, have you been a part of an institution (it need not be "formal") that made you worse? In either case, or both, how did the institution influence you?

THE ROLE OF LEADERSHIP

While associating with better performers has some inevitable performance-enhancing effect, the role of leadership greatly magnifies that effect. Sure, you play better golf with better golfers, and you will become a better person if you spend your time with good people. But these results will more likely be significantly enhanced if your association occurs in an environment designed and maintained to encourage such improvement. John Wooden's players probably would have improved just by playing with each other, but not nearly so much as they did when that association effect was magnified by his coaching.

An organization that wants to maintain a high degree of integrity and a positive ethical atmosphere should do its best to hire people of good character, of course, but the contributions of leadership are critical to obtaining maximum results.

There is no magic formula for leadership in this regard, just as there is no all-purpose procedure for making good ethical decisions. Nor, for that matter, is there any surefire formula for leadership in general—which is not to say that there aren't plenty of books, tapes, and seminars available, many of which are indeed valuable.

The demands and needed characteristics of leadership are too varied and context-specific to be summarized and fit into one simple set of do's and don'ts. The behaviors and traits it takes to excel as a leader of a Navy SEAL team are significantly different—even if some similarities can be found—from those needed to exercise political leadership in a democratic society, and those traits in turn will differ from ones required to effectively lead a multinational corporation. The would-be leader does well to read the books and attend the seminars, and then to sort out the suggestions and strategies that fit his or her context.

> *The demands and needed characteristics of leadership are too varied and context-specific to be summarized and fit into one simple set of do's and don'ts.*

Thus our discussion proceeds with this caveat: the role that leaders can play, the actions they can take, and the policies they can put in place to encourage and enhance the ethical character of their organization will vary from context to context. What will be relevant for some will not likely be so for all.

Additionally, it is important to note that when we talk about the role of leadership in an organization we need not confine our discussion simply to those at the top of the organizational chart. It is common to speak of different levels of management, but it seems a bit awkward to speak of different levels of leadership, even though such a phenomenon exists. (We don't want to get into a sterile debate about the differences between management and leadership. If it seems more appropriate, substitute *management* where *leadership* is used in this discussion.) Depending on the size of the organization, there may be hundreds, perhaps even thousands of people whose job involves some form of leadership.

> ... it is important to note that when we talk about the role of leadership in an organization we need not confine our discussion simply to those at the top of the organizational chart.

ARTICULATION

In many contexts a critical element of leadership is the ability to articulate to an organization's members what that organization is about. The business leader concerned with ethics must do more than merely define the organization in terms of its product or the marketplace (as in, "to be the number one widget maker in North America!"). He or she must also articulate the values of the organization.

The way this is done will vary widely depending on particular situations. In many cases the values of an organization will already have been spelled out, but here, too, situations may differ greatly. Values may be expressed in a simple set of words (*integrity, dependability, honesty*, etc.) that may have been penned by the company's founder decades ago, or they might be represented in a thorough, complex code of ethics and behavior that undergoes frequent revision and updating. Whatever the particular situation, one of the tasks of organizational leadership is to keep those thoughts alive by stating or restating them, by referring to them and—if need be—by explaining them in ways that are fresh and relevant to the times.

> ... a critical element of leadership is the ability to articulate to an organization's members what that organization is about.

This process is common in the political arena. Leaders as ideologically far apart as John F. Kennedy and Ronald Reagan may be best remembered for wielding influence by articulating values as well as for invoking long-held principles and applying them to the situations and context of their times.

Of course, in some cases, a set of values is implicit in an organization, without having been spelled out. This happens in both business organizations and social groups. Certain kinds of behaviors are just "not done," whereas others receive approval and commendation, sometimes subtly. Most of us have had experiences with such unspoken group values, though perhaps not in a business setting.

THINK ABOUT IT . . .

Can you think of an example of a business whose structure implies certain values, even though those values may not be overtly stated? If so, what are the values, and how do the structural elements of the business convey them?

Unspoken values can be learned, no doubt about it, but this is an inefficient and sometimes ineffective way of transmitting a group's priorities to new members. A corporate leader who is concerned about perpetuating the values of the organization will do well to give voice to the traits and behaviors deemed to be important. Not only does it help members learn the values, but it also helps in attracting a certain kind of people.

It is worth mentioning again that these remarks are not confined to those "at the top." In a large organization with multiple functions spread over multiple locations, the words and exhortations of the CEO may simply be too distant to have much effect on, or even get the attention of, employees many layers below. This is not to say that the

> . . . these remarks are not confined to those "at the top."

CEO ought therefore to remain silent about matters of values and principles. Rather we mean to point out that value-emphasizing roles may be needed at a variety of other levels within the company. Touchstone words like *integrity* and *commitment* may refer to principles that are widely understood to be at the basis of the company's character; nonetheless, it may fall to subordinate leadership to explain how those concepts are to be translated into reality for the sales division, engineering, human resources, and other departments.

In concluding these remarks about the need for leadership to articulate organizational values, we acknowledge that many people are understandably reluctant to speak about values, and even more reluctant to take the lead in discussing them. While there might be many reasons for such reluctance, certainly two primary ones are a desire not to appear "preachy" and an uneasy feeling that values are, after all, *subjective* or *relative* and that therefore one should not impose personal values on others.

The latter position has been considered theoretically in Chapters 2 and 3, but the practical issue, even if we grant the premise, is whether or not it is appropriate to impose one's values on others. From the organization's

> *If these values define the organization's character, then they are the values of the organization. Whether they can be "proved" to be ultimately defensible is beside the point.*

point of view the answer is clearly "yes." If these values define the organization's character, then they are the values of the organization. Whether they can be "proved" to be ultimately defensible is beside the point. The point is simple: "This is what we are. Those who would be a part of this organization need to know this, and to know that they are expected to conduct themselves in these ways. People may have every right to live and conduct themselves in other ways. But not here."

As to the first concern, that taking the lead in the organizational value conversation seems uncomfortably "preachy," well, there's one of the burdens—if it is a burden—of leadership. And surely it would not be one of the greater ones. Even more helpful, though, would be to recall a point made in Chapter 3. As a simple matter of fact, we are overwhelmingly more likely to encounter agreement than disagreement about values and principles. So if spelling out company values seems like preaching, at least most of it will be "preaching to the choir." And know that the choir will appreciate that the message is being delivered to those who need to hear it.

THINK ABOUT IT . . .

At whatever level, how can a leader (or manager, if you prefer) talk about values without sounding "preachy"?

IMPLEMENTATION

The leader who is concerned about and responsible for the promulgation of values throughout an organization must not only enunciate those values but also implement programs and practices that will help instill or reinforce them. Again, it is obvious that the specifics of such activities will vary widely from circumstance to circumstance. In some situations, holding periodic discussions or classes dealing with industry-specific ethical concerns might be appropriate. Other situations might call for less formal procedures. The point is that, while it is important to spell out the values of a company, it is not sufficient simply to do that. Leaders must provide ways to bring home those values to the different segments of the workforce and their specific situations.

> *Just as it makes sense to provide task-related training for the sales force, or the fabric cutters, or the middle managers, it makes sense to provide value training for all employees.*

Just as it makes sense to provide task-related training for the sales force, or the fabric cutters, or the middle managers, it makes sense to provide value training for all employees. We would expect the training modes and contents to vary just as different jobs vary. The specifics of what it means to act with integrity for employees in the accounting department and for those in human resources will be quite different.

It is the job of leadership at various levels to devise forms of value training and reinforcement appropriate to their areas of oversight and responsibility. Safety, quality control, and customer service may all be important priorities of a company, but one doesn't expect top-level leaders to devise specific training and systems to enhance these areas. That is a job for those closer to the situation. So, too, with implementing the ethical concerns of the organization.

The discussion and development of codes can be extremely useful in this regard. And the fact that a company may already have a code doesn't preclude the development of, so to speak, "subordinate codes." Indeed, one of the common complaints about codes is that they are so general and vague as to be unhelpful. It may sound nice that a company enjoins all its employees to "do the right thing," but that may not give much guidance to a sales manager who has to settle a dispute between reps over claims to a new customer; nor does it provide direction to the buyer who has been invited by a vendor to enjoy sumptuous transportation and lodging facilities offered in connection with a trade show.

Codes have been discussed more thoroughly in Chapter 3. Suffice it here to repeat both that codes ought never to be a substitute for thought and that they cannot possibly cover every situation. Nonetheless, they may be extremely useful as guidelines tailored closely to job or industry-specific contexts, and they can often give us answers in situations where we have neither the time nor the inclination to engage in an actual or internal moral debate about a preferred course of action.

Finally, while it may be leadership's responsibility to develop and train on codes that help employees understand how to implement the company's values in the context of their own specific jobs, that task is best done collaboratively. Leaders must lead and managers must manage, to be sure. Nonetheless, policies and procedures—be they ethics guidelines or strictly functional ones—will have a much greater chance of acceptance and implementation if they arise out of the knowledge, concerns, and experience of those who will be affected by them. Moreover, if codes are to be useful, they need to be updated to take account of changing circumstances and new situations. No one understands these circumstances better than those on the front lines.

> *. . . policies and procedures—be they ethics guidelines or strictly functional ones—will have a much greater chance of acceptance and implementation if they arise out of the knowledge, concerns, and experience of those who will be affected by them.*

EXAMPLE

It is said that, just as there are three ways to teach, there are three ways to lead: by example, by example, and by example. That's not all there is to it for either role, of course, but the point is well taken. How does this principle apply to the development of values and ethical behavior in a corporate setting? What examples can leadership give that will enhance the moral climate of the organization?

We certainly know what sorts of examples are *bad* in this regard. At the time this is being written, corporate America is reeling from a seemingly endless wave of revelations of unethical and unlawful behavior by top executives in major corporations. The stock market fallout from this news is well known, but a worse and longer-lasting effect is the poisonous cynicism and contempt it breeds among employees. They are liable to take those attitudes with them as they move on to other jobs in other corporations, and if they ever harbored sentiments such as loyalty, respect, and commitment before, it cannot be expected that those will be forthcoming again soon.

> All the codes and value statements in the world become meaningless if, up and down the organizational chart, there is not a continuous chain of individual professional behavior living out the values espoused by the company.

For the most part, though, the character and behavior of board members, top executives, and company owners are not—unless exposed in a negative way—likely to be observed or noted by employees. This is where the role of lower-level leadership is crucially important. All the codes and value statements in the world become meaningless if, up and down the organizational chart, there is not a continuous chain of individual professional behavior living out the values espoused by the company. The sales manager who treats his own staff as merely a means to achieve his personal advancement is not going to successfully instill a customer-first ethos in his department. The finance officer who makes it a policy to put the squeeze on suppliers and to string out payments is not going to inspire those around and under him to go the extra mile for the company. However you interpret the phrase "What goes around, comes around," it seems to hold true.

> If you want to influence those who report to you to be passionate about their work, then be passionate about your work.

When we talk of leadership by example, we don't mean that leaders engage in the same sort of tasks as those whom they influence. If you want to influence those who report to you to be passionate about their work, then be passionate about *your* work. It need not be the same kind of work. Nor are the skills presupposed to be the same. It takes different skills to be a sales manager than it does to be in sales (not that there isn't some overlap). A leader needs to exercise the skills and virtues required of him or her in order to encourage others to do what is required of them.

Reprinted with special permission of King Features Syndicate.

THINK ABOUT IT . . .

"Whatever goes around, comes around." What does that mean to you in the context of an organization and the development of an organizational culture?

CONCLUSION

In concluding the discussion of leadership's role in the development of corporate character, it is worth recalling that the root meaning of *integrity* is *wholeness*. A person of integrity achieves wholeness not only by unifying principle and action, but also by integrating values—not compartmentalizing them. A person of integrity doesn't have one set of ethical values for home and another for the office.

Just as moral values occupy one space on a continuum that includes tastes and preferences, those values that seem merely job-related occupy space on the same continuum as those that are "ethical." There is no divorcing honesty as an ethical concept from the workplace value of doing a job well. It would be naive to think an emphasis on work quality could be unrelated to a commitment to trustworthiness.

It bears repeating that the essential ethical trait consists in respect and regard for others. But this virtue is not confined exclusively to "ethical" issues; it

"Let's not play games, Duberman—every ethics
consultant has his price."

lies at the heart of responsible and professional behavior. It involves returning
phone calls, consulting with subordinates, being prepared, and doing one's
best to meet expectations. The leader who takes on the responsibility of in-
stilling a good work ethic will, at the same time, be teaching ethical work.

Wrap-Up Questions

1. Good leadership will _____ the beneficial effects and influences that
   the members of an organization may have on one another.

   Which word best fills the blank to complete the sentence?

   A. enhance

   B. neutralize

   C. overcome

   D. minimize

   E. All of the above.

   F. None of the above.

2. Suppose that *honesty* and *dependability* are among a company's core
   values. It would be the job of leadership to develop a single company-
   wide training program showing how those values are realized in the

same ways in *every* division, be it research and development, advertising, sales, or production.

True   False

3. Those who lead must have the same jobs and responsibilities as the ones whom they lead.

True   False

4. If a company wants to foster certain values throughout its organization, then it is the job of company leadership to

A. articulate those values.

B. develop programs to train on those values.

C. be examples of those values at work.

D. All of the above.

E. None of the above.

5. One reason why it is difficult for companies to teach or encourage ethical behavior is that the character traits that constitute ethical virtues have little value in the world of business.

True   False

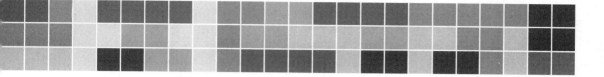

Index